St. Francis
and the Christian Life

St. Francis and the Christian Life

A Disorderly Parable of the Epistle to the Galatians

APRIL LOVE-FORDHAM

With a foreword by Jon M. Sweeney
Art by Kit Fordham

RESOURCE *Publications* · Eugene, Oregon

ST. FRANCIS AND THE CHRISTIAN LIFE
A Disorderly Parable of the Epistle to the Galatians

Disorderly Parable Bible Study Series

Resource Publications
An Imprint of Wipf and Stock Publishers
199 W. 8th Ave., Suite 3
Eugene, OR 97401

www.wipfandstock.com

PAPERBACK ISBN: 978-1-5326-3634-9
HARDCOVER ISBN: 978-1-5326-3636-3
EBOOK ISBN: 978-1-5326-3635-6

Manufactured in the U.S.A.   DECEMBER 11, 2018

*This book is dedicated to Giovanni
and to all those who have the desire to serve God.*

I, Brother Francis, send greetings to you, Brother Anthony, my theological superior. I am pleased that you are now teaching sacred theology to our brothers providing one thing: As it says in our Rule, please see that you do not squelch the spirit of prayer and devotion in them as they undertake studies of this kind.

—FRANCIS, LETTER TO BROTHER ANTHONY OF PADUA, 1224[1]

1. St. Francis, *Francis of Assisi in His Own Words*, 71.

Contents

Foreword

I DO NOT KNOW April Love-Fordham very well, but I have known of her love for Francis and Clare since the days of the pilgrimage with her husband, Steve, that gave birth to this book. I remember in 2014 April messaging me along the Camino di Assisi, exuberant in what the two of them were seeing and experiencing.

This is a beautiful book. April's descriptions of the Umbrian countryside and towns evoke a timelessness many of us associate with Franciscan spirituality. I can smell the olive trees and feel the breezes on mountain passes in the scenes that April paints. More importantly, she does here what we desperately need spiritual books to do: she prompts questions in us, as readers, in ways that help point us, as fellow pilgrims, in the direction of answers.

"What question do you walk with?"

That's what one enigmatic friar asked April and Steve early on in their journey. I found myself returning again and again to this, almost like a still point. I still am returning to it, after I've finished April's book.

In her own searching for answers, April explores the letter of St. Paul to the Galatians. She went to Italy, and made her way to Assisi on Francis's feast day, pondering St. Paul. His teaching in that epistle, his own personal transformation, and the history of his leadership in the early church, are shown to be relevant to April's own answer to the old friar's question on the road. She answered him with a certain sense of urgency, "How are we to live the Christian life?"

How, indeed.

Central to the juxtaposition of Paul and Francis throughout St. Francis and the Christian Life is the way in which each of them responded to God's grace, listened for the Spirit, and utilized moral guidelines and rules. In a most gentle way, through anecdote and conversation, April offers insight into what living Christianly means, leaving us much to ponder—because, as all of us understand who sincerely and deliberately try to be Christian, this is all much tougher than it sounds.

Common and essential to both Paul and Francis were their very personal encounters with Christ. They heard God speak to them. I often wonder, were people such as these special recipients of that particular grace, or were they simply able to pay attention in ways that we don't. Paul's encounter with God took place at the start of the church, and Francis's renewed that church twelve hundred years later.

Somewhere in the personal God-relationship is the key to everything that matters. Paul had visions. Francis danced and sang. They each responded to their Lord with exuberance, but also with the most everyday sort of ordinary faithfulness.

I rarely do.

They each met Christ in ways that affected them physically. Paul of course went blind, and then later, experienced "marks" of Jesus on his body from what he suffered. Francis likewise underwent what we have learned to name as stigmata on Mt. La Verna. These are mysteries, as are all our lives with Christ.

April wrestles with all of this, to our benefit. Her conclusions are not always the ones I'd arrive at. At times, she wrestles with Francis and his methods of faithfulness in ways that I might not. But the conversations she provokes are always relevant, and I found myself listening carefully to whatever she had to say. Her method of conversation-learning is such that I could almost imagine her sitting with Clare and Juniper and Anthony of Padua at San Damiano, talking about what it means to love God and follow Christ in faithfulness.

What are we to do, now? That might be my answer to the old friar's question on the road.

"There is no formula with the Spirit," the same friar tells April by the fourth and final part of her book, and that's what I'll take away most. Surely that is why the God-relationship is the most important thing of all.

—**JON M. SWEENEY** is the translator/author of *Francis of Assisi in His Own Words* and *The St. Francis Prayer Book*, and the fiction series for children, *The Pope's Cat*. He lives in Milwaukee with his wife and daughters.

Photographs from April's pilgrimage to Assisi appear in *The Complete Francis of Assisi* (Paraclete, 2015), which Jon Sweeney edited, translated, and introduced.

Preface

In the fall of 2014, my husband and I embarked on the trip of a lifetime through the Italian wilderness, retracing the final footsteps of St. Francis into Assisi. At that time, we had many questions about where God might be leading us after we returned to our lives in Atlanta, Georgia. We hoped that by spending those weeks in prayer, we would receive some very specific answers. This book is the story of what became a most unexpected journey into both the life of St. Francis and the lessons that the Apostle Paul teaches in the Epistle to the Galatians.

WHAT IS A DISORDERLY PARABLE?

Jesus used parables—stories of everyday people—to illustrate spiritual truths. His parables were about everyday people and everyday things. However, they were not nice, tidy stories. They were subversive and meant to challenge things that the listener thought were truth, but were not. *St. Francis and the Christian Life* is my and my husband's story—a parable of everyday people that illustrates the spiritual truths found in the Epistle to the Galatians. My goals for this book are threefold. First, I hope it will challenge you to question what you thought you knew about living the Christian life. Second, I pray the Holy Spirit will use it to increase your desire to live the Christian life. Finally, I hope you will find answers about living a Christian life that is uniquely yours.

THE DISORDERLY PARABLE BIBLE STUDIES

St. Francis and the Christian Life is the third book in the Disorderly Parable Bible Studies series. The first was *James in the Suburbs* (2014) on the Epistle of James and the second was *Dismantling Injustice* (2016) on the Song of Solomon. Each book stands alone and the series does not need to be read in any order.

SPIRITUAL PRACTICES

This book is divided into four parts. At the end of each part, there is a suggested spiritual practice to try. They are designed—as the Apostle Paul explained in Galatians—to help us "sow to the Spirit."[1] Like most spiritual practices, it is good to work on one at a time—maybe over several days or weeks—until you believe the Holy Spirit has finished speaking to you through it.

GROUP STUDY

If you are studying this book with a group, then you may find the section called "Lesson Plans for Study Groups" useful. It divides the book into twelve group meetings and offers questions that will jump start group discussions.

INDIVIDUAL STUDY

If you are studying this book by yourself, you may still enjoy the questions in the section called "Lesson Plans for Study Groups." Try journaling the answers after you finish each chapter. Then put a note on your calendar six months out to return to them and see how the Spirit has worked in your life.

1. Gal 6:8.

Acknowledgments

I WOULD GRATEFULLY LIKE to acknowledge the following people who have played a significant role in the writing of this book and in walking alongside me on my journey to live out the Christian life.

My team of advisors who read the first draft together and spent a month of Wednesday nights eating my cooking and sitting in my living room discussing it. You are the best friends I could ever have! I love each of you so much. Ron Bagwell, Becky Beal, Sharon Fordham, Pat Klausman, and Victoria Jarvis. The book is what it is because of you!

Jon Sweeney, whose writings about St. Francis and careful interpretations of ancient documents, including St. Francis's own words, continue to inspire me. Thank you for bringing St. Francis to life for me long before I traveled to Assisi. Your work is a gift to us all!

Sue and Arnold Shives, our Canadian friends who we met walking St. Francis's last steps. How wonderful it was to share stories, blisters, rest days, and magnificent dinners together in the Italian wilderness! I have always felt that your presence was a gift from God.

Headwater Holidays, who arranged our self-guided hike, following in the footsteps of St. Francis—especially Lisa Gillman and Helen Hodson.

My family, who are a never-ending wonderful! Brent Fordham, who worked tirelessly as editor and resident theologian. Kit Fordham (artkit. co), who made this book complete with his illustrations. Chanelle Gallagher, who inspires me with her wisdom to rethink things I once ignorantly took for truth. Maggie Mayhem, my awesome Great Dane, who sits by the window next to my desk watching for squirrels, deer, and birds—quick to warn me when the neighbor's cat comes for a visit.

My discernment groups, both of which have been a remarkable blessing to me! Colleen Bast, Ron Felder, Rose Patrick, and David Simmons. Tom Erdmanczyk, Lia Bertelson, Jeff Bailey, Marjorie Garrett, Lee Hunter, and Robbie Stadter. Sister Barbara Young for being my Spiritual Director and helping me find courage to face the unknown.

Dr. Chuck Campbell and Dr. Stan Saunders for exposing me to St. Francis for the first time during that splendid Gospel Foolishness class in seminary. We started each class by dancing our hearts out . . . sometimes even on our desks! "What kind of fool are you?" you asked us. You taught us that a holy fool is one who has died to the world so much so that it no longer matters what the world thinks about them, making holy fools uniquely qualified to deliver God's message to the world. I long to be a holy fool because of the two of you!

Finally, to my brilliant and wonderful husband Steve Fordham, who I love more than all the stars in the Assisi sky! Thank you for everything. Hiking, editing, brainstorming, and always making me laugh. It's been grand!

PART 1

Rest and Restlessness

1

Pilgrimage to Assisi

My husband and I woke to cool dry air drifting into our open windows along with the morning sun. The second floor of the cream ashlar farmhouse had original pine hardwood floors and roughhewn ceiling beams.[1] We would be spending the next four weeks here. My husband would be taking a desperately needed rest, and I would be making gentle progress on research for a fortnight class I would be teaching the following spring. Unbeknownst to me, my work would eventually proliferate, although not overnight, into this very book.

Our tired legs had been hiking for exactly eleven days on the Cammino di Assisi.[2] We'd been staying mostly in refuges offered by churches and monasteries along the way. We felt a profound sense of accomplishment at this, our second to last stop before completing the pilgrimage. This was a planned detour between Valfabbrica and Assisi. This *agriturismo* was a working organic farm whose specialty was oil from the Leccino olive tree. In fact, the rows of olive trees we could see from our windows were filled with olives. The harvest would begin in just a little over a month.

Assisi was only a day's hike away, but we had planned to take a month's break from the trail and finish our pilgrimage into Assisi on the eve of St. Francis's feast day. The *agriturismo*, with its comfy king size bed and

---

1. See picture 1 in the appendix.

2. For anyone who would like to hike the 187 mile Cammino di Assisi, the journal *Walking the Cammino di Assisi* (2017), by John N. Merrill is highly recommended. The website, www.camminodiassisi.it, is also helpful.

spacious *en suite* bath complete with an antique claw-footed tub and separate shower, was a luxurious step up from the community sleeping quarters and sleeping bags we had been crashing on for the past eleven days. Oh, and don't let me forget the smell of homemade bread wafting in from the kitchen of the farm building attached to ours via a modern glass breezeway. It was all an indulgent delight.

Yet, we couldn't stay under the vintage *matelassé* comforter too much longer. Today was the celebration of the Cavalcata di Satriano—a reenactment of the dying Francis's final return to Assisi. We had a two-mile uphill walk to get back to where we had passed the Satriano historical marker on our hike in the evening before.[3] The marker had a serious but enchanting warning: "Wayfarer who approaches this place, do it in the silence of the mind and in the peace of the heart."

The marker memorialized the place where the *cavalieri,* or knights, had stopped for dinner with the blind and dying Francis in tow. We wanted to get there a bit early so we could stand where we could get some good photographs of the reenactment. The Knights of Assisi, on their way home from fetching Francis in Nocera Umbra, were to pass through on horseback about half-past noon.

The climb was uphill and hard, not because it was truly difficult, but because we had just walked 177 miles and were exhausted. Though we would occasionally pass a house and could see a farm here or there in the distance, this was considered the edge of the Italian wilderness. We saw no cars and no animals except for a flock of white ducks, who had befriended a longhaired white dog and were lounging together on the white stone *strada.* Not a human being was in sight. When we reached the ridge, we could see Rocca Maggiore, the larger of the Assisi castles, sitting five miles away in the distance, sandwiched in the dip between the towering Mount Subasio and the Umbrian hills. Hiking this ridge as the sun was setting behind Assisi on our way in the night before had been spectacular. Like a cloth dip dyed in the colors of the rainbow, the sky transitioned from light blue to yellow to peach to pink to purple. Then as the sky touched the mountain, Assisi sat where it had sat for more than two thousand years wedged in safety between the rising hills. Soon we passed another *agriturismo* and spotted the historical marker just ahead and a sign pointing us to La Cappella Satriano, a very tiny but sturdy stone chapel set in a clearing in the woods.[4]

---

3. The Satriano historical marker and chapel are located at 43 06'18.4"N 12 42'36.6"E.

4. See picture 2 in the appendix.

I looked at my husband and he looked at me. We were the only ones there. As we thought about it, we concluded we were indeed in the middle of nowhere so how had we ever expected a crowd would turn up? Nevertheless, the brochure said the knights would pass by Satriano in thirty minutes and there would be a Mass. Well. We plopped down on the middle of the three stone stair steps leading into the one room open niche and reread the brochure.

It wasn't long before we heard a rustling in the undergrowth beneath the craggy green trees and for the first time noticed a narrow, unpaved path in the woods leading to the chapel. Towards us walked a Franciscan. Later my husband would refer to him as an "old school" Franciscan. He had on a tunic, but it wasn't the rich brown one we had seen on every other Franciscan we had met on our journey. This one looked more like a faded burlap sack—not the kind Marilyn Monroe had modeled in support of the Idaho potato. No, this one was far less form fitting and had been patched uncountable times. Presently, it was splitting at the side seam above his ankle and could use some work. Covering his shoulders was a mantle made of the same material with a hood sewn onto it. Around his waist was a white cord. He had a beard and bowl cut hair streaked with gray. He carried a sling bag made of blue fabric over one shoulder. And he was barefoot. Where his feet weren't dirty, they were notably ashy and dry.

The friar's gait was peppy—almost dance-like. He smiled and then bowed deeply upon reaching us. It was such unusual behavior that, in retrospect, it made us both a little nervous. In unison, we got up from the steps and stood aside making way for him to enter the chapel. But it wasn't the chapel he was interested in it. It was us.

"*Buongiorno!*" he sang out as he reversed his swan dive and stood in perfect mountain pose. No yogi could have mastered the asana better. Looking from one of us to the other with eyes wide and hopeful, the little lines around his eyes crinkled. He grinned ever larger at our muteness, making us even more suspicious that perhaps he was not all there.

My husband was the first one of us to speak. He held out his hand and offered a *buongiorno* back. Then apologized with *purtroppo, parlo molto poco Italiano*. It wasn't quite true. My husband, after having his DNA tested and discovering he had Italian roots, had actually spent many late, but short, lunch breaks sitting in his clients' cafeterias learning Italian from an app on his phone. My husband is a linguistic genius. The talent extends to software languages too. Hence, his profession of computer programmer has been perfect for him. At any rate, he had learned Italian and according to his app was now 93% fluent. Right now, however, he just didn't want the challenge of keeping up with this odd little character in the woods.

"But I speak English," the little friar offered again almost singing it out with palms up outstretched toward us and no hint of an accent.

Rattled, neither of us asked how he knew we spoke English or where he had learned the language or how he came to speak it so clearly without even a hint of an accent. Or even where he had come from. Or why he was dressed so strangely. Honestly, it felt like we had met a garden gnome who had come out of the forest to entertain us.

"What are you doing here in Italy?" he asked.

"We've been hiking the Cammino di Assisi," I answered.

He rolled his arm flapping his hand in the air as if we owed him more of an answer than that. Neither of us was certain we should say anything to this man, but in the awkward moment of silence that followed while we tried to get our bearings, I was the first to give in.

"We're taking a rest break until the eve of St. Francis's Feast Day when we'll complete the journey into Assisi. I'm working on a series of lectures on the Apostle Paul's Epistle to the Galatians." While not taking my eyes off the monk, I motioned to my husband to encourage him to tell his part of the story.

"I'm going to actually rest!" my husband declared. "After all, that is what vacations are for." Though my husband had started out as a software developer, he had long ago moved into a position of technology consultant where he is in front of people all day long instead of hiding behind a computer. Moreover, he had been working fifty hours a week leading his software teams and getting his clients' business systems built, installed, and up and running. The work was rewarding even though the constant human interaction took him out of his comfort zone. He and I were both long overdue for a vacation.

"And right now? You are here to see the cavalry—the Knights of Satriano?" queried the man.

We were indeed. He asked if we knew their story. We had read a little, but for better or worse, we encouraged him to please tell us everything.

So the little friar sat down in the grass and motioned for us to sit back down on the steps. There he told the story starting in the year 1226. Francis, in his mid-forties, was suffering from a variety of maladies. He had gone to the village of Nocera Umbra to try and ease his stomach aches with the city's renowned mineral water. But as other more deadly ailments caught up with him, he came closer and closer to death. The people of Assisi heard this and sent the Knights of Assisi to bring him home.

"I understand the people of Assisi loved Francis dearly," I stated more as a question than a fact.

"Yes. They did and at first glance it might seem it was their love of him that brought him home, but in truth, they wanted to make certain they would possess his body at his death, believing it would bring glory to Assisi."[5]

"Treasuring the relics of saints is a very foreign idea to Protestants," I inserted, giving away the fact we were not Catholic.

"It shouldn't be. Not if you read your Bible," he shook his finger at me as he hopped up dramatically. While still pointing his finger at me, he lectured, "The remains of Elisha, the prophet, resurrected the dead man who was put into his tomb when his body accidently touched Elisha's bones.[6] And Paul's dirty laundry healed sick people just by touching it.[7] The shadow of Peter healed the sick when he passed by them.[8] The honoring of relics is very much based on the stories of scripture. You must have faith!" His eyes stared into mine checking to see if he had convinced me.

As I was unable to get my words out, my husband touched my knee and with a wink said, "You know he's right." Neither of us felt a need to argue.

The friar emitted a long deep breath showing his concern. Then, deciding it mattered not, he went on.

"It turned out after a day's ride, the knights arrived in Nocera Umbra. The next day, they gently placed Francis on horseback to bring him home. After traveling all morning, they came to the very place where we now sit called Satriano."

With that, a shiver went up my spine making the hairs on my arms stand up. To think Francis had sat here. I looked around me and tried to soak up the feeling of the place. The trees, though mature, were quite short and shrubby. We were close to the edge of the ridgeline with a valley far below. It was almost silent. The birds were probably as taken aback by this

5. Sabatier, *The Road to Assisi*, 144.

6. 2 Kgs 13:21.

7. Acts 19:11–12.

8. Matt 14:35–36, Mark 6:56, and Luke 8:43–44.

man as we were. I closed my eyes and slowly inhaled in order to smell the scents around me. It smelled fresh and pure.

"Of course, the chapel was built in memory of the occasion and wasn't here at the time Francis arrived," the little friar continued. "Well, the knights were famished from traveling for a day and a half. They badly wanted food. So they left Francis here on a blanket in the short grass while they scoured the whole area, finding absolutely no food for sale at any of the farms they visited."

After some time, the Knights of Assisi returned empty-handed to find Francis on the blanket with all kinds of food surrounding him. Francis told them that one, then two farmers had passed by and seeing what he needed, shared what they had. The knights, astonished, asked if they might have a bite or two. But Francis admonished, "You didn't find anything because you trust your flies[9] more than in God." He told the knights, "Go back to the houses you have visited, offering the love of God instead of money, and humbly beg for alms![10] Don't be embarrassed. After sin everything is bestowed as alms, for the Great Almsgiver gives to the worthy and the unworthy with kind piety."[11]

Becoming more and more hungry, the knights overcame their embarrassment and went begging alms. That day the knights, as well as the villagers, learned one could buy more with the love of God than with money.

When the little friar seemed to have completed the story, my husband, still not feeling entirely comfortable with the happy, bouncy little man, waved our brochure in the air, trying to match the friar's enthusiasm while attempting to confirm we were in the right place, "So today the modern Knights of Assisi reenact their retrieval of Francis?"

"Yes. They will be by." The friar's demeanor grew quiet and he sat back down on the ground. "Well, has your pilgrimage on the Cammino di Assisi provided any spiritual insights?"

"Not yet." I answered, allowing my disappointment to show, then added, "Though it has been very pleasant, our prayers and meditations have not yet produced fruit."

"What question do you walk with?" He listened for an answer as if we were his only concern in the world, as if he had been waiting for us to reach this spot all of our lives just so he could ask us this question. It was eerie and

---

9. Francis often referred to coins as "flies" indicating his disgust for money.

10. The word alms means money or food given to poor people.

11. Celano, *The Francis Trilogy*, 216.

silly all at once. He made me nervous, and, yet, I liked him—trusted him too. I must have. Here I was about to tell a total stranger about our lives.

"How are *we* to live the Christian Life?" I looked into the friar's eyes hoping he had an answer. He rolled his hand like he had before, indicating he wanted to hear more.

"Well, we were both in need of a good long vacation," I started out.

"You know pilgrimages aren't exactly vacations?"

"Yes. That is why we did the pilgrimage—or most of it—before this long break we are just starting. We both love our jobs, our church, the ministries we are involved in, but we needed a rest. Because we were particularly worn out as of late, at first we thought our pilgrimage question would be how we could find peace in our busy lives. But as we studied that idea, we realized what we were asking was really larger than just finding a way to get the needed rest so that we would be enthusiastic about the things we already love doing."

"Very astute! The peace Francis spoke of was not about scheduling in a time to relax—like, perhaps a massage on Saturday mornings or taking a walk during a lunch break at work. He had this incredible desire for the world to know true peace—the wholeness found in Christ."

"Exactly," I said.

"So," my husband joined in, "as we thought about it, what we really wanted to know was how one lives the Christian life. In most ways, our lives are very much like our neighbors' lives—on one side of us, there is an African-American family who claim no religion at all. They are fine people with great children. They are some of our closest friends. On the other side of us, our neighbors are Hindu. Again, both neighbors are fine people we even trust with the keys to our house. We all go to work, spend time with our families, hang out with our friends, and volunteer our time to good causes. Yet, *we* claim to be followers of Jesus. What does that even mean to us? Shouldn't we at least approach life in a Jesus kind of way? Like we've been praying, 'How do we live the Christian life?'"

I added, "We want to wake up every day knowing we are part of something beyond ourselves—something more important than our own ambitions—something that will give us lasting satisfaction and inner peace."

"Even if it's difficult or a challenge, we want to pursue God's will," my husband said with determination.

"Marvelous question!" cried the little friar and he clapped his hands in delight. Then we all stared at each other. Did the friar have an answer? If so, none came.

Eventually, I became uncomfortable with the silence and added, "That is why we are here. We hoped St. Francis had some answers we could discover. As you most certainly know, Francis gave up all material possessions. For him, this was the key rule to living the Christian life. We admire him very much, but how can *we* follow this command of Jesus? If we give all we have to the poor, what then? We can't live under a bridge or in a dilapidated church—nor can we beg for all of our food. So how are *we* to live for Christ? Are we missing a key piece of theology? Do we need to do more good works? Is there a set of rules we need to follow?" My tone begged for an answer.

When the friar still didn't answer, my husband summarized, "Simply put, how do we follow Jesus?"

"I see," the little friar said with a smile and then he whispered, "St. Francis got a lot of things right, but not everything."

He jumped to his feet again distracted by the sudden sound of the approaching footsteps of half a dozen horses. The Knights of Assisi in historical attire with details perfectly reproduced from the thirteenth century, rode up to the chapel, disembarked from their gallant horses, and knelt—each on one knee in the grass in silent prayer. No one spoke. When they mounted their horses again, the little friar ran alongside them yelling, "the Great Almsgiver gives to the worthy and the unworthy with kind devotion!" and then disappeared from sight. When they were gone, my husband and I were left alone still sitting on the steps of the chapel.

"What was that?" I asked, astonished.

"That was an odd little friar and a bunch of Satriano reenactors?" my husband laughed.

"Did you get pictures?"

"No. I was distracted. You didn't get any either?"

I shook my head no.

Getting back to our *agriturismo* was easy. We crossed back over the ridge and the rest was all downhill. The white fuzzy dog followed us most of the way barking in a friendly voice. When we passed the house the dog had been at earlier, this time a cat was lying with the ducks.

My husband motioned toward the cat. All I could think to say was, "My goodness this is a strange place."

When we got back to the farmhouse we each, with a book in hand, planted ourselves on a comfortable couch in the reception area where a large weaving loom took center stage. The weaver was absent, but a rug was partially woven still on the loom.

After a while, the hostess, a young woman with short red hair appeared. We had encountered her the night before when our stopping to watch the sunset from the ridge meant we had to make the rest of the hike in the dark,[12] but she gladly met us at the farm's outer gate to let us in and show us the rest of the way. Now she asked if she could get us a drink and if we enjoyed our morning. "Did you make it to the Satriano Chapel?" she asked.

"Yes. But we were the only ones there," I replied. "The knights rode by dressed out in full costume." Pulling the bi-fold brochure, which I was now using as a bookmark, out of my book, I looked at it closely, "Look, the brochure says the Cavalcata di Satriano is at 'ore 12.30 Arrivo a Satriano con Liturgia Eucaristica.' What did we get wrong?"

My husband elaborated. "We weren't exactly the only ones. This little old school Franciscan Monk showed up."

"Was the monk *insolito*?" inquired the hostess.

"Unusual," translated my husband.

"Yes!" we answered together amused to hear him described that way.

"I believe you have been blessed to have met Brother Giovanni! He is *mistico*."

"He was a bit unusual, but I wouldn't call him mystical," clarified my husband.

"Perhaps not, but when I saw the *cavalcata* leave the Rivotorto[13] yesterday morning—as I have every year since I was a child—the knights were riding in twentieth century street clothes—not costume. They wore riding helmets. There are a few women who ride now too. One rider was even sharing his saddle with a little black dog. Unless I am mistaken, you've experienced something mystical—or maybe shall we say—unexpected?"

"Giovanni was there," I added as evidence nothing unusual had happened. As soon as I had said it, I realized how ridiculous and meaningless that sounded.

12. See picture 3 in the appendix.

13. *Rivotorto*, which means winding river, is now the site of a neo-gothic church built over two stone structures where the Franciscans first found shelter. It is located outside the Assisi walls in the valley below. In ruins at the time of Francis, the brothers dubbed it the *sacro tugurio* or holy hovel.

My brow furrowed and my husband sat up straight in his chair. "I know what we saw."

"Of course," she conceded. "If you want, you aren't too late to make it to the Piazza del Comune to see the *carroccio* lead the knights into Assisi. I could find someone to drive you."

"What is a *carroccio*?" asked my husband.

"Two white cows pulling a cart with the Bishop of Assisi standing on it leading the knights through town. First they go to the Piazza del Comune. In the hands of the bishop is a gold reliquary with a relic of St. Francis inside. From there they go to the *piazza* in front of the Basilica di San Chiara where they honor St. Clare, Francis's friend and confidant, with a tribute of flowers, and finally to the Basilica di San Francesco."

"Do you want to go?" I asked my husband.

"I will if you want, but I liked our plan to wait until the Feast Day of St. Francis to see Assisi for the first time. It's time for me to read a book and rest."

"As you wish," answered the hostess. "Enjoy your afternoon!"

While she worked at the reception desk for a few more moments, my husband and I exchanged glances. We wanted to process all she had just told us, but were too embarrassed to do it while she was in earshot. She seemed perfectly fine with us having experienced something *mistico*. But we weren't from Assisi and we weren't used to the unexpected being normal.

Her work ended at the reception desk, and she picked up fresh white towels to deliver to one of the bedrooms. She started toward the heavy wooden door, then turned back to us, "I want to put your minds at peace. You should know Brother Giovanni is one of God's jugglers bringing joy and wisdom to those who meet him.[14] There is nothing to worry about for he is as wonderful as he is harmless. You have been blessed!"

---

14. Francis nicknamed the Franciscans, "The Jugglers of God" after asking the question: "Is it not in fact true that the servants of God are really like jugglers, intended to revive the hearts of humanity and lead them into spiritual joy?" Sabatier, *The Road to Assisi*, 136–137. A recommended devotional book that celebrates this aspect of Francis is *The St. Francis Holy Fool Prayer Book* by Jon M. Sweeny (Paraclete Press, 2017).

2

Creating a Community
Galatians 1:1–2

FOR THE NEXT FOUR weeks, we recuperated in the Umbrian countryside. The autumn temperatures made the *agriturismo's* pool too cold to swim in, but halfway up a hill and across a small grey-brick bridge, we found two woven beige lounge chairs with tiny flat roof-like awnings that protected our heads from the sun. We spent many afternoon hours curled up in them watching quarter-sized Roman snails crawl across our footrests.

The skies became a brilliant blue and fluffy white clouds floated by. I have evidence of this, because I snapped picture after picture of these fluffy cloud formations. Their forms, which would have gone unnoticed had we not achieved our tranquil Zen-like state, now captivated me. This was the most rest we had ever had in our entire lives. We were the only guests except for the weekends when young families would take the train two hours north of Rome into the countryside to teach their children about farm animals. Other than that, it was gloriously quiet.

In the mornings, I would go to the farm's chapel where the sun shone through its abstract stained glass windows. It was an attractive little one-room stucco building with a grand arched double wooden door. A twelve-pointed star spanned both doors with Hebrew letters above each point representing the Hebrew calendar. In the chancel apse, there leaned three tall icons against the wall—Mary, Jesus, and St. Francis. There were no pews, but on the beautifully polished wooden floor lay large flat pillows where one could sit and meditate. Just inside the entrance of the chapel on a lectern sat a cathedral-sized Italian Bible. I noticed every morning, though I never saw another soul in the chapel, the pages would be turned to the daily gospel lectionary while the two attached ribbon bookmarks marked the daily Psalm and epistle readings.

I would bring my laptop and prop myself against a wall using two of the floor pillows. There I would study Galatians using my collection of commentaries and the papers of famous scholars—some of them centuries old—that resided on my Kindle and are now part of the bibliography of this book. Galatians itself started with:

Paul an apostle[1,2]*—sent neither by human commission nor from human authorities, but through Jesus Christ and God the Father, who raised him from the dead—and all the members of God's family who are with me, to the churches of Galatia. (Gal 1:1–2)*

Galatians was an epistle, a letter written to instruct its recipients. It was the earliest known letter authored by Paul, about seventeen years after the death of Christ. He dictated all but the last few verses, which were written in his own hand.[3] The name and bio of Paul's stenographer was unknown, but we know Paul was presently among other believers. The epistle's recipients were an early gentile Christian community Paul had founded in Galatia, an area in the highlands of central Anatolia in modern Turkey. In the letter, Paul was angry at outsiders who were disrupting the community's precious and intimate relationship with God. Hence, Paul poured out his frustration in searing, passionate words.

Paul had a progressive vision of community even by today's standards. Prior to becoming a follower of Jesus, he had been a member of the Jewish sect called Pharisees, a serious rule following group who believed strongly God had ordained a superior Jewish nationalism. The Pharisees nurtured feelings of superiority over all other races and nations. Every morning, the

---

1. The word apostle, translated from the Greek *apostolos*, meant ambassador or messenger. It was sometimes used as a title either of the original twelve disciples or other leaders in the early church, but it was also used as a descriptive calling rather than a title. The accepted church leadership did not recognize Paul or give Paul the title of Apostle. However, he used it anyway because Christ gave him the directive to be an ambassador to the gentiles in Acts 9:15.

2. Because Paul lacked the equivalent of ordination credentials, N.T. Wright humorously dubs him "a second hand apostle"—at least in the collective minds of the early church leaders. Wright, *Paul for Everyone*, 4.

3. Gal 6:11.

men of this Jewish sect woke to prayers in which they thanked God they were not gentile dogs, slaves, or women.[4] Until his transformation, all of Paul's life had centered on being part of this Jewish community of Pharisees, who maintained they alone possessed the correct theology to believe, a holy list of God-given religious rules to keep, and a compulsory set of good deeds to do. All of which they avowed were necessary in order to be right with God.

However, when Paul met Jesus and became part of the Jesus movement, the Spirit led him to open up the movement—even leadership positions—to gentiles, slaves, the poor, and women.[5] Therefore, this early Christian community in Galatia was being set free from the unjust systems of the world (or what Paul called "the present evil age") [6] to follow the way of Christ.

Paul was not the first Jewish convert to reject Jewish nationalism along with its customs and religious rules. In fact, prior to his conversion, Paul, who was then called Saul, had held the coats of his friends and mentors as they stoned Stephen, a young deacon of the Jerusalem church. Paul heard with his own ears the charges against Stephen: "For we have heard him say this Jesus of Nazareth will destroy this place and will change the customs Moses handed on to us" (Acts 6:14).

Stephen's death no doubt left a mark on Paul. You see, the Pharisees weren't so much worried about whether Jesus was the Messiah or not. They didn't believe he was the Messiah, but they could tolerate that claim as long as those who subscribed to it also kept the Jewish way of life. What they couldn't let go of was their nationalistic pride. They could not comprehend why Jewish Christians were inviting unclean gentiles to become part of the Jesus movement and letting them enter the Jewish holy places to worship alongside Jews. Therefore, the Pharisees and other likeminded Jews decided to wipe out this progressive Jesus movement altogether.[7] Paul was a young leader in the anti-Jesus movement and persecuted Jewish Christians even to the point of stoning them.

However, after his conversion, Paul founded the communities in Galatia on the conviction Jesus had set humanity free from following religious

---

4. Today these prayers are a part of the *Birkhot haShahar* or *The Dawn Blessings*. The first recorded version appeared around 200 A.D. in the Talmud Menachot 43b.

5. Gal 3:28 and Col 3:11.

6. Gal 1:4.

7. Acts 6:1—8:2.

rules of any kind—including those set forth in the Torah.[8] As I was to discover later in Paul's letter, not only would the Galatian followers of Jesus no longer keep their pagan rules and rituals, but there would be no participation in Jewish customs and religious rules either. Instead, the Holy Spirit would lead the community.

These wealthy, educated pagan gentiles eagerly joined with Paul.[9] In fact, after hearing the gospel, they stopped worshiping their pagan gods,[10] acknowledged there was only one God,[11] and eliminated discrimination.[12] Paul had taught them they "belonged to Christ,"[13] were "children of God,"[14] and were "heirs of God's promise."[15] Most importantly, they were people of the Spirit, living and guided by the Holy Spirit.[16]

Unfortunately, this vision of Paul's was controversial even in the early church. The early church, most of whom were ethnically Jewish, hadn't been entirely convinced that to follow Jesus one didn't have to be—or at least become—Jewish. It took the majority of early Christians, including the leaders and the apostles, a long time to get rule following nationalistic Judaism out of their systems. Nevertheless, Paul wasn't waiting for them to get on board. He was actively establishing communities that had been set free.

This disagreement between Paul and the other leaders inevitably raised concerns about Paul's legitimacy as an apostle or even as a follower of Christ. Paul addressed these concerns by simply stating at the very beginning of his letter that he was "sent neither by human commission nor from human authorities, but through Jesus Christ and God the Father."[17]

---

8. The Torah is the law of God as revealed to Moses and recorded in the first five books of the Old Testament. It includes the Ten Commandments and hundreds of other rules governing all aspects of Jewish life.

9. Betz reasons, "The fact that Paul wrote his well-composed and, both rhetorically and theologically, sophisticated 'apology' forces us to assume that he founded the Galatian churches not among the poor and the uneducated but among Hellenized and Romanized city population." Betz, *Galatians*, 2.

10. Gal 4:8–10.

11. Gal 3:20 and 4:6.

12. Gal 3:28.

13. Gal 3:29 and 5:24.

14. Gal 3:26.

15. Gal 3:29.

16. Gal 4:6 and 6:1.

17. Gal 1:1.

Paul expanded on the question of his credentials later in the epistle, but for starters, he wanted the Galatians to remember what he had taught them came directly from the resurrected and ascended Jesus. Jesus said, "But the Advocate, the Holy Spirit, whom the Father will send in my name, will teach you everything, and remind you of all that I have said to you" (John 14:26).

It was through the Holy Spirit—the Spirit who Jesus promised God would send—that people who were free from religion and its long list of rules got their guidance. It was where Paul got his guidance. He was not ashamed when others did not agree with him.

All of that was unfolding before me as the sun from the eastern sunrise poured into the apse of the farm's little chapel. Even as a child, one of my passions had been to hear the stories of Scripture. So having this time to be quiet, to read, and to meditate was priceless; but several days a week, my husband and I would leave the *agriturismo* and venture into Parco Monte Subasio for a day hike with a picnic in tow.

It had been about two weeks since our arrival when one day we decided to venture all the way to Eremo delle Carceri, which literally means "hermitage of the prisons." The decision was made while my husband was brushing his teeth the night before.

I said, "Wanna hike to Eremo delle Carceri tomorrow?" Perhaps it was my poor Italian or more likely he was in denial that he had hearing loss, but what he heard was "Wanna hike to Elmo's Cave?"

"Elmo's Cave?" he laughed.

"*Eremo?*" I corrected, but too late. Forevermore he would taunt me by referring to the sacred hermitage of St. Francis as "Elmo's Cave." Even to this day. And it never gets old.

It was a four-hour hike each way so we started out the next morning, before the farm animals were awake, with a picnic breakfast and lunch stashed in our daypacks. The jovial chef at the *agriturismo* promised a hearty dinner would be waiting for us in the kitchen upon our return that evening.

The hike through the Italian wilderness was spectacular. At times, we would get long-distance views to the south and could see Assisi sitting peacefully in the distance. We caught glimpses of hang gliders floating between the hills in the thermals above us. We stopped to take pictures of them with the blue silhouette of Assisi in the background. We crossed a medieval bridge that spanned a deep ravine, which a babbling creek below had worked centuries to cut into the rock. An orange and black tabby cat, who wanted the scraps from our breakfast, followed us. Afraid it would follow us all the way to Assisi and get lost from the farm it belonged to, we eventually decided to scare it away.

We had been warned there was an aggressive pack of wolves in the area as of late and stayed on the lookout, but if they were there, we never saw one. Mostly, we thought about what this must have been like in the days when Francis walked this trail. How he must have interacted with the birds and animals. How easy it would be—surrounded by such remarkable beauty—to offer praise to God with each step. Small wild flowers dotted the path where rays of sun had worked themselves through the trees. Queen Anne's Lace, wild orchids, and a pink flower, which I did not recognize, were the most common. Where the trail was exposed, several different types of yellow flowers grew in abundance.

As we grew near to Assisi, nature had littered the trail with fist-sized white marble stones. Even with our well-heeled hiking boots, it was not the easiest surface to walk on, but eventually the trail came to a road and ahead of us a cross crudely made from fallen trees marked the path to the back entrance of the hermitage. We had been told not to take the path to the back entrance, even though it was quite close, because the back gate was always locked. So we took the road down the mountain to a paved entrance. The buildings of the hermitage had been built over the small cave (or "prison" cell) where Francis would go to get away from the world and pray. The website of the hermitage, which we had consulted for opening times and directions, had explained the word "prison" was a way of describing a place to "voluntarily segregate one's self from the world in order to allow God through silence and prayer, to find a free space in one's heart."[18]

To the north of the wide tree-lined path at the entrance to the hermitage was the rising forested slope of Monte Subasio towering above us. To the south was a spectacular view of the valley below and hills beyond. An indescribable sense of tranquility filled the fall air. Neither of us spoke as we walked the final path to the monastery paved with packed down marble gravel so common in these hills.[19] We passed two Franciscans in their spotless dark brown linen tunics tied with a white cord, known as a cincture, and brown leather sandals that might have been Tevas. The cinctures had

18. *Provincia Serafica dei Frati Minori dell'Umbria.* "*Eremo delle Carceri* – Assisi." www.assisiofm.it. www.eremodellecarceri.it (accessed June 1, 2018).

19. See picture 4 in the appendix.

three knots tied in them meant to help the brothers remember their vows of poverty, chastity, and obedience. The two friars were leaning against the short stone and stucco wall on the valley side of the path having a quiet discussion. They smiled and gave us a welcoming nod as we passed. Then up ahead coming toward us, we were surprised to see Giovanni in his tattered sackcloth and glowing smile.

Upon spotting Giovanni, my husband mumbled the theme from the 1960 television series *The Twilight Zone* only loud enough for me to hear it, "do-Do-do-Do." I couldn't help but laugh. The very human Giovanni recognized us immediately and waved.

"Brother Giovanni?" my husband asked and offered an outstretched hand, as we got closer.

"I see my reputation has proceeded me once again. Someone has told you my name!" He seemed genuinely excited to see us and inquired, "You have come to Assisi two weeks early?"

"Not exactly, this is as close as we are getting to Assisi today," I answered. "We hiked here this morning to visit Eremo delle Carceri." I pronounced it correctly and looked at my husband daring him to call it "Elmo's Cave" in front of Giovanni.

"I see. Would you like a tour?" he offered.

Would we like a tour? We were thrilled to have a tour! About three hundred yards further, we descended through a short arched tunnel with two signs hanging above our heads. One said *Silenzio,* commanding silence from us as we entered. The other contained the Latin words *Ubi Deus ibi Pax* or "Where God is, there is peace."

The tunnel opened into the courtyard of the hermitage.[20] In silence, Giovanni, thrilled to be showing us this sacred place, lifted his arms and turned 360 degrees. It was clear he was telling us to pause in the radiant sunlight and enjoy the view of the valley below and the rising mountain behind us. After a few minutes of taking it all in, he led us behind what looked to be an ancient well from which the monks had once drawn water, but now served as a container for a batch of glowing red geraniums. We entered into a small arched door. Over the door there was a symbol of the rising sun with the letters JHS—*Jesus Hominum Salvator* or "Jesus, Savior of Humanity."

Inside we stood in a primitive stone room. Giovanni whispered to us that this room was an early structure—a twelfth century oratory—that

20. See picture 5 in the appendix.

Francis and his earliest followers frequented. It was much later when the structure was incorporated into the present day building. Through two chapel-like areas and down a steep narrow staircase, we came upon a plaque pointing down a few steps further: *Grotta di S. Francesco.* We entered a tiny chamber carved out of the Monte Subasio bedrock.

In silence, Giovanni knelt on the cave floor now paved with bricks. We followed suit although it soon brought pain to both of our knees. This was once the cave Francis would come to in order to spend time alone with his creator.[21] The small cave walls look plastered and I suspect reinforced, but it still felt fusty. Other visitors followed us in just a short time and we were compelled to leave so they could experience the space too.

Upon exiting onto the sunlit terrace, we saw the *Buco del Diavolo,* or Hole of the Devil.[22] It was a small quatrefoil shaped hole in the terrace. I had read about this hole. It covered a once deep crevasse into which Francis tossed a demon who was tempting Brother Rufino, one of the early Franciscan friars now buried with Francis in the basilica. Rufino had been having visions of Jesus speaking to him from the cross. However, the message Jesus was speaking was not edifying and so it was obvious that the vision was of a demon only pretending to be Jesus. This fake Jesus had told Rufino that Francis and all of his followers were damned. Francis suspected that something was wrong, so he called Rufino to come to him. He told Rufino the next time the devil spoke to him, to chase the devil away by saying, "Open your mouth and I will empty my bowels into it." Rufino obeyed. It worked. The demon flew into the crevasse causing an avalanche that filled the crevasse with rocks from Monte Subasio. Years later, when the proper hermitage was built, the quatrefoil shaped hole was placed there as a memorial to Brother Rufino, who never again saw the fake Jesus, but only the true Christ who affirmed Rufino with, "You did well, my son. The devil depressed you, but I am your Christ, and from this day forward, I will never allow you to be depressed like that."[23] From that day on, Rufino was always filled with joy and peace of mind.

Giovanni ignored the quatrefoil hole and led us across a bridge to the rustic gardens that covered the side of the mountain east of the hermitage. He pointed us to Brother Leo's, Brother Masseo's, and Brother Rufino's

---

21. See picture 6 in the appendix.

22. See picture 7 in the appendix.

23. Brother Ugolino, *The Complete St. Francis,* 292.

caves. Then stopping at an outdoor stone altar with a bronze tau[24] bolted to it, we sat down. Breaking our silence, we began to talk.

Brother Giovanni, much less bouncy than our first encounter, but not at all sedate, explained that Francis and the friars talked about these little caves as containing "a great and valuable treasure." His eyes lit up at the word treasure. Then he leaned in toward us, as if about to reveal a great secret. "The treasure, of course, was that they had found a place where they could talk to God in secret—a place where they could seek the Kingdom of God."[25] Giovanni also pointed out that Jesus had said the Kingdom of God was "like treasure hidden in a field."[26]

"Or in this case, a cave," snickered my husband.

"Yes, they came here to be in the presence of God. The presence of God is the purest definition of the Kingdom of God, wouldn't you say? Francis's companions said at times it was such a place of transformation for Francis that 'one person seemed to have entered, and another to have come out.'"[27]

When Giovanni was satisfied we had gotten his point, he inquired of me, "How are your studies of Galatians coming along? Are you learning much about Paul and the Galatians?"

"Yes! And thank you for remembering!" I smiled. "Perhaps it's because I'm in the Umbrian hills and am surrounded by St. Francis while I study, but I'm finding a lot of commonalities between Francis and Paul. For instance, they both started Christian communities. And though their visions for the communities were quite different, both of their visions became very unpopular with the church. Even today, the church has twisted the visions of both men in order to conform them to something palatable and controllable."

24. Brother Sean of the Tau Community of Saint Francis writes that the Tau Cross was adopted by Francis after hearing Pope Innocent III preach on Ezek 9:4–6 on November 11, 1215. The Pope interpreted the passage to say that those who repent are marked by an angel with the sign of the tau (the last letter in the Hebrew alphabet). The Pope saw this as the foretelling of the church being marked with the sign of the cross. The tau then became a medieval sign of repentance and transformation. Francis began painting it on the walls and doors where he stayed and used it as his signature on some of his writings. He also adapted his tunic to the shape of a tau. Brother Sean, *History of the Tau Cross*, 1–5.

25. "But whenever you pray, go into your room and shut the door and pray to your Father who is in secret; and your Father who sees in secret will reward you." Matt 6:6.

26. Matt 13:44.

27. Celano, *The Francis Trilogy*, 27.

"So you know a lot about St. Francis?" Giovanni asked.

"Not really," I answered honestly. "I've read several books, but I am no expert. Anything you might teach us would be welcome."

That was all the encouragement Giovanni needed. "Then let's talk about Francis's community!" Thus we began.

Just as Paul had started several communities in Galatia in the first century, Francis had also started several in and around Assisi in the 13th century. There were the Friars Minor for celibate men (today known as the Franciscans) and the Minoresses for celibate women (also known as the Poor Clares). In short order, he would also start a lay order for families and others (known as the Third Order Franciscans).[28]

Francis, like Paul, claimed his vision for these communities came directly from Jesus himself. Jesus spoke to Francis in 1209 during Mass at the little Chiesa di Santa Maria degli Angeli.[29] The priest read from the words of Jesus recorded in the Gospel of Matthew:

> Jesus said, "As you go, proclaim the good news, 'The kingdom of heaven has come near.' Cure the sick, raise the dead, cleanse the lepers, cast out demons. You received without payment; give without payment. Take no gold, or silver, or copper in your belts, no bag for your journey, or two tunics, or sandals, or a staff; for laborers deserve their food." (Mat 10:7–10)

But during the reading, something happened before Francis's eyes. It was no longer the priest reading these words. He saw Jesus standing in the place

28. The Third Order Franciscans are still active today and include separate orders for Catholics, Anglicans, Lutherans, and an ecumenical order. Each offers a formation process for men and women wishing to make a commitment to the rule of St. Francis while continuing their secular vocations.

29. The names used to describe the area where this event happened are not used consistently in the literature and have changed over time. The little church was first called Chiesa di Santa Maria, but over time took on the name Chiesa di Santa Maria degli Angeli because locals had reported the singing of disembodied angels coming from the dilapidated church set in a forest grove in the valley below Assisi. Documents of the City of Assisi have references to the church dating back to the year one thousand. Sabatier describes it as "one of those rare spots in the world on which rests the mystic ladder that joins heaven to earth" (Sabatier, *The Road to Assisi*, 42). Francis took it upon himself to repair the church, which was soon to be given to the Franciscans along with "a little portion" or *porziuncola* of land surrounding the church. Today the Chiesa di Santa Maria is referred to as the Porziuncola and sits inside the Basilica di Santa Maria degli Angeli along with the Transito, the Franciscan infirmary, where St. Francis died. It is interesting to note that three California cities, Los Angeles, San Francisco, and Santa Clara, get their names from the three basilicas in Assisi.

of the priest speaking directly to him. These words were transformative for him—a command he would diligently follow for the rest of his life and would institute in the communities he founded.

Giovanni stood and looked intently at us with his eyes dancing and said, "Francis suddenly knew how he was to live the Christian life. He had been asking the same question you are asking on your pilgrimage!"

Giovanni once again became the animated little garden gnome we had met at Satriano. He decided to act out the rest of the story using the words of Francis: "That day in the Porziuncola, Francis cried out, 'This is what I want! This is what I was seeking. From this day forth, I shall set myself with all my strength to put it in practice.'"[30]

From that day forward, Francis determined to strictly obey this Jesus-given rule of life. Jesus had called him to proclaim the good news and help others while rejecting material things.

It was not long until friends of Francis, named Bernard and Peter, decided to join him in following this rule of life. So one day, after going to early morning Mass in the Church of St. Nicholas,[31] the three approached the altar and Francis read those words from the Gospel of Matthew to them.

Giovanni raised his arms to sky and quoted Francis, "Brothers, this is our life and our Rule, and the Rule of all who may join us. Go then and do as you have heard."[32]

It seemed irreverent to ask practical questions of Giovanni after that hallowed performance. It was obviously something near and dear to him. So we sat quietly together listening to birds chirp until it felt right to speak. Finally I half asked, half stated, "I've learned that a Rule of Life is something more formal than just a way of living."

"It is what one signs up for when one takes Holy Orders," responded Giovanni. "But in the beginning these words of Jesus were the only Rule of Life these budding Franciscans had or wanted."

"So it is a list of rules you promise to keep?" I clarified.

30. Sabatier, *The Road to Assisi*, 43–44.

31. The Church of St. Nicholas was a Romanesque style church located in Assisi's main square. It was built in the 2nd Century, but destroyed by an earthquake. The Assisi post office, city offices, and information center now occupy the area where it once stood. This church is not to be confused with the Chapel of St. Nicholas that is located in the lower Basilica of St. Francis.

32. Sabatier, *The Road to Assisi*, 46.

"I guess you could say that. They are a commitment to live your life accordingly. Some orders are very strict about adherence and others take it more as guidelines. Francis was really very strict."

So that was how Giovanni described to us the birth of the Friars Minor. Francis's vision was that his community would serve Jesus without owning property. As the Rule of Life became more formal, Francis specified the brothers were not allowed to even touch money except in rare circumstances, much less have any money.[33] They could each own two tunics (one with a hood and one without), pants, and a belt made of cord. They would help everyone who came to them in need, but rather than charge for their work, they would beg for their own food. At first, Francis allowed those who could read to have a prayer book, but eventually he would rethink even that. As time went on, there would be a few other rules they agreed to follow as well.[34]

For Giovanni and my husband, I summarized what I was thinking so far, "It sounds like to me that Paul and Francis had very different visions for their communities. For instance, Paul did not institute religious rules in the Galatian community. He didn't insist upon voluntary poverty, or doing a set of good works, or even following Jewish law. His desire was that the Spirit alone would guide the Galatians."

"Yes," Giovanni answered. "Francis, on the other hand, believed his rules, especially the rule of poverty, to be a necessary part of the Christian life. He believed the friars, and others, should work hard to keep these rules. After all, Jesus said, 'If you wish to be perfect, go, sell your possessions, and give the money to the poor, and you will have treasure in heaven; then come, follow me.'[35] And also 'Be perfect, therefore, as your heavenly Father is perfect.'[36] Unlike Paul, Francis thought the Spirit would not guide him or his community if they didn't first meet the criteria he thought Jesus had set."

---

33. St. Francis instructed the brothers not to touch money with the exception of when it was required to care for a sick brother—perhaps to buy medical items or pay a doctor. If they found money, they could not pick it up. If they were begging for food and were offered money instead, they could not take it. St. Francis, *Francis of Assisi in His Own Words*, 28–30.

34. The Franciscan's First Rule and the Rule of Life for the Third Order Franciscans is found in the following book: St. Francis, *Francis of Assisi in His Own Words*, 17–41.

35. Matt 19:21.

36. Matt 5:48.

"Back to Paul . . . Paul's vision of community set the followers of Christ free from 'the present evil age'—from religious rules and unjust systems—so they would be free to be guided by the Spirit," I posed.

"Yes. But Francis's vision of community put in place a set of rules designed to set the follower free of the desires of the flesh—material belongings, money, sex, and other such things—so they would be free to serve God, others, and even creation," reflected Giovanni.

My husband added, "So they both experienced freedom in their conversions, but in a different way. Paul was freed from religious rules while Francis put some religious rules in place that were meant to free him from the desires of the flesh. However, they both did what they did for the same reason. Both wanted to serve God."

Giovanni and I both nodded our heads in agreement and Giovanni laughed, "Absolutely. But we are not the first to see their similarities and differences. Francis's biographer, Paul Sabatier, wrote, 'There is hardly anyone, except St. Paul, in whom is found to the same degree (as St. Francis) the devouring need of being always something more, always something better, and it is so beautiful in both of them only because it is absolutely instinctive.'[37]

I then added, curious if Giovanni had come to the same conclusion, "And yet, I believe they would have disagreed with one another quite passionately!"

"That is for sure!" With that Giovanni bowed, backed away from us, and skipped. Yes, skipped! Down the path and into the forest he went as he waved goodbye to us.

"Well, at least he didn't just disappear this time," I mused.

"Oh yeah, this is a lot better than last time," declared my husband sarcastically as he stood, stretched, and looked around the forest garden wondering if anyone else had seen the strange little man.

---

37. Sabatier, *The Road to Assisi*, 43.

3

Finding Freedom
Galatians 1:3–5

Two weeks later, we had had a long rest, and I had gotten a satisfying amount of work done, but we could have easily been convinced to stay another month. It had been idyllic. However, it was time to leave our *agriturismo* and hike into Assisi on the eve of St. Francis's feast day.

We followed the trail of the Cavalcata di Satriano—the trail the knights used to take the dying Francis home to Assisi.[1] The landscape varied from tall, thickly forested trees to canyons to arid ridges to glorious vistas exposing vineyards, sheep and goat farms, and olive groves. The long hike ended in a fairy tale scene as we rounded the side of Monte Subasio and began to catch glimpses through tall trees of Rocca Minore, the smaller of the two castles that guard Assisi. There the path ended at an imposing medieval gate that interrupted the smooth lines of the ancient city walls in order to welcome us in. This was the back door to Assisi and the gate the Knights of Assisi carried Francis through.[2] I imagined it looked much the same as it did that day in 1226 minus the paved road.

The gate was permanently open so we slipped through unnoticed without another person in sight. It was invigorating to make our way through the pleasant cobblestone streets and townhomes of Assisi and to see it being decorated with garlands and flags in celebration of St. Francis.

1. See picture 8 in the appendix.
2. See picture 9 in the appendix.

Official events were to start that evening. Our bed and breakfast was on Via Sant'Agnese. As we navigated the narrow streets, we slowed down and took in the ambiance. We passed three old men who sat gossiping on out-of-place white plastic chairs on a quiet street too constricted for cars.[3] They each offered us a friendly *ciao.* In the open door behind them, we could see old women, perhaps their wives, in simple Italian dresses preparing food in the kitchen. The residents of the ancient townhomes, which sat directly on the street without benefit of a front garden, took pride in decorating their windows and stair rails with colorful flower boxes, most of which held flourishing red geraniums.[4]

Too tired to visit it now, I noted an *antichita,* or antique shop, set into the side of the Cathedrale di San Rufino. Then coming out of a long tapered passageway, down a ramp, and through a small tunnel, we found ourselves turning to look at the front of the Cathedrale di San Rufino. This cathedral was where Francis had been baptized as an infant. Next to it, on the left, a small sign on the wall indicated this was also where the childhood home of *Santa Chiara,* or St. Clare, once sat. At eighteen years of age, Clare had been one of the early followers of Francis and eventually became the Abbess of San Damiano. There she led his female followers, who also rejected materialism. Sleeping in an open-air room, they devoted themselves to manual labor, silence, and prayer. Clare came from a noble and wealthy family. Her home would have been quite impressive, but nothing remains of it today.

After another short jaunt down a narrow lane, we descended stone stairs, which were so old they had hollows carved into them from a million footsteps before ours. It was there we found ourselves in Piazza del Comune, the largest square in Assisi.[5] The square, with its simple fountain, was filled with people dining *al fresco.* The aroma of food was hanging in the air while hanging from the window sills were red banners, marked with the heraldic lion of Italy, alternating with blue banners, marked with a simple cross. Festive lights, flags, and flowers decorated every corner. At the far end of the *piazza,* we could see the Santa Maria sopra Minerva—the Roman Temple of Minerva—built in the first century and more recently recycled into a church. The Torre del Popolo, the clock tower, loomed above the square on the far side of the temple.

---

3. See picture 10 in the appendix.
4. See picture 11 in the appendix.
5. See picture 12 in the appendix.

"Let's go get a shower and come back here for our own *al fresco* dinner." I emphasized the words *al fresco* hoping to show him I was not completely illiterate in Italian.

"Okay, but you should know Italians don't use *al fresco* to mean dining outside."

"Seriously? What does it mean?"

"Literally, 'in the coolness.'"

"So they might take it to mean I was asking for an inside table out of the sun?"

"No."

"Then what?"

"It refers to spending time in jail. Maybe they would have thought you wanted dinner in jail," he answered laughing at me, then added, "I wish I had let you ask for an *al fresco* table to see what would happen."

"I bet you do! Good for me, you are a slow thinker!" spoken as I intentionally bumped into him with my shoulder. To which he bumped back harder than intended, slightly knocking my backpack and me into a stranger, forcing him to offer apologies to us both. No one was hurt and like kids we were happy to be together in this amazing atmospheric place.

After walking down Via dell Arco dei Priori for a bit more, passing Francis's childhood home housed as part of Chiesa Nuova, and taking a right (instead of what we learned later should have been a left), we stopped in a small, mostly paved square to check directions. My husband got out his map and called out our location, "This is Piazza del Vescovado. Our lodgings for the night are back the other way, but right around the corner."

"Piazza del Vescovado?" I asked wide-eyed.[6]

He shook his head yes, as he set his backpack down next to a stone fountain topped with a pinecone finial.

"But it is so insignificant compared to Assisi's other *piazzas*," I exclaimed.

"What were you expecting?"

"Doesn't *vescovado* translate into bishop?" I said smartly, recovering from my most recent language *faux pas*. "This is the bishop's square!"

"One of these was a manse? Nice digs!"

"This is where one of the most pivotal events in Francis's entire life happened! I would've thought there'd at least be a plaque." However, it was more like a parking area. It held a small twelve-by-six foot slightly raised

6. See picture 13 in the appendix.

area separating traffic. The raised area, where we now stood, held the small fountain.

While my husband took advantage of the fountain and filled up his water bottle, I went on explaining that on that pivotal day in Francis's life, his father, Pietro di Bernardone, was angry with him. Perhaps he was frightened for him too. Francis's behavior looked unstable to his father. In fact, Francis's whole personality had changed. Pietro's only son had been one to carouse and party with his friends, but now he had become a sad recluse spending his days alone, often at one of the churches in or around Assisi. He had once been interested in the family merchant business, which dealt in cloth, and in working alongside his father, but had lost all interest. Pietro was not the only one to notice the change in Francis's personality. The children of Assisi had even taken to calling Francis *pazzo* or madman for his unkempt appearance. There had been a recent incident where the children had thrown stones and mud at Francis until he had broken down and cried in front of them.

"So his dad was a kind man, worried about his son?" asked my husband.

I started to explain, then said, "Come with me. Let me show you something we just passed. I thought we'd save it for another day, but it's so close. Come . . . I will explain."

It was a short two-minute walk retracing our steps to Chiesa Nuova.[7] As we entered the little courtyard in front of the church, I brought him around to where he could see the statue labeled *Al Genitori di S. Francesco*—The Parents of St. Francis.[8]

"This church is attached to and built around Francis's childhood home and there's ma and pa!" I giggled. "What do you see in this work of art?"

"Interesting!" My husband stroked his beard slowly, pretending to be an art expert. Looking the statue over, he ruminated aloud on what he saw, "They are holding hands—sort of. Truthfully, his hand is wrapped around hers. He is grasping *her* hand, but she hasn't responded in kind. She is holding a broken chain in the other hand. I believe this must signify there is something wrong between them. He looks determined. Like his mind is made up. Like he knows what is what. Yet, he is not happy. She is looking away from him. Her expression looks kind, but unsure."

---

7. See picture 14 in the appendix.
8. See picture 15 in the appendix.

"Isn't it a great statue?" I interrupted. "Notice they're both dressed very well." Moving closer to the statue to get out of the way of a tour group of Franciscan monks who were exiting the church, I playfully went on, "Let me introduce you to Pietro di Bernardone and his wife, Mona Pica." Then I bowed and waved my hand in introduction.

"You've been friends long, have you?" my husband played back.

Pietro was a successful merchant—an importer of fabrics—and had been hopeful his son would one day take over the family business. In fact, over one of his arms was draped some fabric. In the days leading up to the event in Piazza del Vescovado, while Pietro had been out of town on business, Francis sold his father's inventory in order to finance the restoration of San Damiano, an old church located just outside the city gates.

Excited about getting to see what I had only read about, I tugged on my husband's shirt cuff, "Come inside with me."

We stepped inside the church and stood still while our eyes adjusted to the darkness. To the left, I could see set into the stone of the house—perhaps under what was once a staircase—a half-height stone closet with a metal lattice door.[9] Someone had lit the small compartment and set some artificial flowers in it.

"That's it!" I said to my husband. "Pietro was so worried and angry and embarrassed by Francis he locked him in there to keep him off the streets! That is why his mother is holding the broken chains. Mona Pica couldn't stand her son being confined so when Pietro was away from the house, she freed Francis, risking her husband's temper."

"So there was friction at home! Pietro was not a kind man."

"Correct. When Pietro arrived home, not only had his inventory and profit from its sale disappeared, but now his son was gone too! Pietro, angry, prone to violence, and no doubt certain that his son had gone mad, approached the bishop to adjudicate the situation between Francis and himself. Pietro wanted desperately to get custody of his grown son to avoid further embarrassment."

We were both tired so I suggested we walk back to Piazza del Vescovado and onward to our bed and breakfast while I finished the story instead of exploring the rest of the church and family home. When we got to the Piazza del Vescovado, I began again, "At the appointed time, the bishop, Pietro, and Francis, along with a large crowd of nosey looky-loos, met in this square."

9. See picture 16 in the appendix.

"Right here at this fountain?"

"Maybe," I guessed.

Upon hearing Pietro's complaint against his son, the bishop instructed Francis to return his father's property—whatever remained of it. This did not dismay Francis as expected. In fact, he was filled with joy. Francis obeyed and gave his father everything—all of the money in his pockets and every bit of clothing he was wearing. Naked, Francis then denounced his father, "Until this time, I have called Pietro Bernardone my father, but now I desire to serve God. This is why I return to him this money, for which he has given himself so much trouble."[10]

After which Francis left Assisi by the nearest gate wearing only a servant's cloak provided by the bishop. For the first time in his life, he experienced freedom—freedom from materialism, freedom from his father's harsh demands. He experienced freedom *from* and freedom *to*. He had been set free to serve God without constraints.

Though much of the town thought Francis had indeed gone mad, the anger and lack of compassion demonstrated by his father gave everyone a deep sense of sympathy for Francis. After all, these people had known Francis all his life and, even as a carousing playboy, he had always endeared himself to them.

I concluded the story by explaining, "In this square was Francis's first encounter with freedom from the materialism that had enslaved his father. It resulted in an all-encompassing, unfamiliar joy extending over him and he expressed his gratitude to God by running through the forest and fields singing praises to God."

We sat down on the stone pavers around the small fountain, leaning on our backpacks. We sat quietly while an occasional car disrespectfully drove around our little fountain platform on its way through town, breaking our meditation, but we just wanted to soak it all in.

After a while, my husband broke the silence and whispered, "So in this square, Francis gave up everything—his family, his inheritance, his way of life!" The full weight of what that meant hit us both. This was no altar call where someone comes down and prays a prayer then goes back home to life as usual. This was literally giving up everything to follow Jesus.

Then my husband asked our pilgrimage question, "How are we supposed to live the Christian life?"

---

10. Sabatier, *The Road to Assisi*, 39.

"I don't know. I'm too tired to think about it." With that, I stood up and nudged us down the road to our bed and breakfast.

With very little effort, we found our bed and breakfast, built during the heart of the crusades. The exterior was a light pink-beige stone, also like all of the other townhomes in Assisi. The city was simply stunning, right out of the middle ages, lovingly maintained by villagers and Franciscans alike. The arched entrance door to our bed and breakfast was up four stairs and opened into a common room with beamed ceilings. Our room, with tall windows mounted above our heads, on the very top of the building, was *splendido* as advertised. Best of all, it was warm and a private shower greeted us. While my husband showered, I unpacked my computer and read over the notes I had been taking on Galatians.

Like Francis, Paul had given up his old way of life to follow Jesus. He too described what he gave up as finding freedom.[11] However, what Paul gave up was different from what Francis gave up. Francis gave up material things, a life of comfort, a life of parties, and upper middle class wealth—all things Paul would later lump into what he called "the desires of the flesh."[12] Francis joyfully gave these up to pursue doing God's work of repairing old churches, caring for the poor, spreading the story of Jesus, teaching others to live in servitude and peace, doing miracles, healing the sick, and even honoring nature as God's glorious masterpiece. He had been set free *from* materialism and set free *to* follow Jesus. Put another way, Francis found freedom from the desires of the flesh—the chief of which, for him, was materialism—and he did so by deciding to follow a list of religious rules that he found in the teachings of Jesus.

Paul saw things differently. He gave up his way of life as a devout Jew, a rule following Pharisee, and an up-and-coming Jewish leader. He had followed a set of rules, some of which were found in the Old Testament and some of which were developed by the Pharisees. But now he was giving up all of those rules. In addition, Paul cut ties with Jewish nationalists. When Paul found Jesus, he found freedom from religion and its rules. He had been set free *from* a long list of rules and set free *to* be guided by the Holy Spirit. As a significant side benefit of being guided by the Spirit, Paul found he had also been delivered from the desires of the flesh.

---

11. "For freedom Christ has set us free." Gal 5:1.

12. "Do not gratify the desires of the flesh." Gal 5:16.

Paul obviously also gave up considerable material comforts in order to travel into gentile territory to start Christian communities[13]—sometimes working as a tent maker in order to pay his own way.[14] In addition, he taught his communities to give of their resources to the poor.[15] However, Paul was never focused on voluntary poverty or even living simply as being a fulfilment of the Kingdom of God. Paul never demanded his communities give up all of their material belongings to follow Jesus. He gave no indication voluntary poverty was necessary to follow Jesus.

So it was not an issue of freedom from materialism when Jewish Christian leaders showed up in Galatia. Instead, they were demanding the Galatians adopt the Jewish religion first—including following their rules and customs—in order to follow Jesus. This was abhorrent to Paul and the result was that Paul wrote the Epistle to the Galatians in protest. As we will see later, he did not limit his protest to their directive to follow Jewish religious rules. Paul believed following any religious rules would enslave those who followed them. Francis would have disagreed. Francis felt Jesus had left us with a new set of rules to follow and he handed these down to the Franciscans.

I had come to believe Paul would have seen Francis as mistaken. He most likely would have seen Francis's determination to promote a list of rules as misguided and he might likely have written Francis the same letter he wrote to the Galatians. I imagined it would have gone something like this:

> Dear Francis, Instead of teaching your men to follow a set of rules, teach them how to follow the Spirit. Only then will your men be free. Lovingly, Paul

Of course, my imagination was much kinder than what Paul actually said to the Galatians. He was in protest mode. But his letter didn't start out in protest. It started with a beautiful blessing of "grace and peace."

---

13. "Poor, yet making many rich." 2 Cor 6:10.

14. Acts 18:3.

15. "They asked only one thing, that we remember the poor, which was actually what I was eager to do." Gal 2:10.

> *Grace to you and peace from God our Father and the Lord Jesus Christ, who gave himself for our sins to set us free from the present evil age,[16] according to the will of our God and Father, to whom be the glory forever and ever. Amen.[17] (Gal 1:3–5)*

Paul got right down to business. He had to. The gospel had been distorted and Paul would not let that stand. Paul reminded the Galatians that Christ had set them free from "the present evil age." For Paul, "the present evil age" was religion and culture. Any religion or any set of religious rules, which all in one manner or another seek to control God and our relationship with God, was wrong. Culture that allowed unjust systems to regulate how and if people could use the gifts God had given them was wrong. Paul believed Christ had set us free from sin, from guilt, from disgrace, from desires of the flesh, from pleasing people, and from any and everything that had not been put forth by the Spirit. Later, Paul writes, "Now the Lord is the Spirit, and where the Spirit of the Lord is, there is freedom."[18] Paul found freedom by being in relationship with Jesus through the Holy Spirit—not by following a list of rules.

For Francis, on the other hand, "the present evil age" was the desires of the flesh—materialism, lust, hunger, even sleep—but it was not freedom from a set of rules. He believed he had been freed from materialism so he could keep a set of rules he believed were from Jesus.

Nevertheless, as brothers in Christ, separated by more than a millennium, Paul and Francis would have agreed that the point of freedom was to follow Jesus with everything one has.

When my husband had showered, I took my shower and then found him sitting on our tiny terrace carved out of the roof. The lodgings were simple and uncluttered with terracotta floors and wooden beams, but the linens and towels were luxurious. The place was marvelous. Like many of the buildings in Assisi, our bed and breakfast had been built around 1100, before Francis was even born. Italians like to recycle their buildings. This one had even older roots with its foundation on top of a first century Roman villa complete with a few Roman mosaics and columns still visible on

---

16. "Set us free from the present evil age" is similar to "Deliver us from evil" found in the Lord's Prayer.

17. "God *our* Father and the Lord Jesus Christ" and "*Our* God and Father" emphasizes that Paul's communities were united around not just the belief in Jesus as Lord, but also the belief in a common Father God.

18. 2 Cor 3:17.

the lowest floor. Our room was on the top—the fourth floor, if you counted what I would call the basement. From our only window, we could see the bell tower of the Basilica di Santa Chiara.

"I want to know what you are thinking." my husband asked.

"About?"

"Are we supposed to stand in the square back home, strip down to our skivvies, and give up all we have like Francis?"

"Skivvies? Really? I can't believe you just said skivvies." I teased him. Then I got serious. "I suspect the answer is no, because there's very little strategy for living after that. Imagine how that would go back home."

"You mean after our kids bailed us out of jail for indecent exposure?"

"Which one do you think would come get us?" I laughed. "Seriously, where would we live? How would we get food and prepare meals? If we become a burden on those around us, then how can we possibly serve them?"

"Exactly! How does having absolutely nothing benefit the Kingdom of God?"

"I don't think it would. But here we have Francis—the most beloved saint of all time. He thought it was necessary—he thought Jesus had told him personally—to give up material things in order to live the Christian life. If he got that wrong, then how are we ever going to get it right?"

Together we thought about it for a moment: How does one live the Christian life? This was not a question we were asking lightly. Then I blurted out, "You know who I'd really like to talk to about this?"

"Let me guess. Giovanni?"

"Yes," I answered gingerly. My husband chuckled as if we were both crazy while I explained I was serious. My husband did not disagree.

Despite his oddness, Giovanni seemed to be an expert on Francis. We knew very little about Giovanni except that the inhabitants of Assisi—well, at least the hostess at our *agriturismo*—thought he possessed some kind of mystical powers and was a blessing to those who encountered him. We had assumed he was a Franciscan, but he dressed far more primitively and didn't wear shoes. Perhaps he was from a more devout sect than the mainstream Franciscans we were seeing around town. I had heard there were several splinter groups. Some were determined to follow Francis's first rule to the letter, while others had become more progressive. There were other dividing lines too, but I didn't remember what they were. At any rate, we had been too polite to ask Giovanni frank questions about himself and instead had spent our time with him soaking up all he had to say. For all we knew, the man was an absolute *pazzo*.

"Do you think we can find him again?" I asked.

"Something tells me *he* will find *us*. I just hope we don't wake up one morning with him standing in our shower!"

With that, we used one of our smart phones to make a reservation for dinner in a little restaurant set into one of the city walls. Because it was the eve of the Feast Day of St. Francis, we should have made reservations months ago. But we snatched their last seating of the day. We had a table above the city wall overlooking the valley. In the valley sat the Basilica di Santa Maria degli Angeli. Dinner took us through the stunning orange sunset until the lights of the basilica were lit in all of their glory. Then a great surprise awaited us upon exiting the restaurant. Large oil lamps lining the walls of Assisi had been lit. Flames of light encircled the entire village, winding their way all the way up to Rocca Maggiore, the big ancient castle overlooking the town. It was simply breathtaking as pilgrims like ourselves, nuns, and Franciscans quietly strolled the cobblestone streets enjoying the mystical autumn evening.

We noticed a small group of Franciscans were standing on several benches peering into the valley below. We stopped to see if we could catch a glimpse of what was captivating them. One jumped down from the bench and insisted I take his spot. It took a minute for me to understand what I was seeing. In the distance, a procession of hundreds of pilgrims carrying candles was headed into the Porziuncola.

"*Mozzafiato!*" the friar declared to me.

I looked at my husband to see what *mozzafiato* meant. He replied, "Breathtaking!" And it was.

Holding hands and walking slowing back to our bed and breakfast, we passed the Piazza del Vescovado fountain again. My husband asked, "I wonder where Francis spent the night after he ran that day from this *piazza* into the fields?"

"In a ditch," I responded with a smile.

"You're making that up!" he pulled my hand toward him so he could look in my eyes to see if I was joking.

"No. I really am not making it up. It was early spring and snow was still on the ground. He ventured—singing at the top of his lungs—into an area of the forest known to be inhabited by robbers and thieves. Whether he knew they had set up camp there or not is unclear. But they confronted him by asking who he was. Still swept up in ecstasy, he answered that he was 'the Herald of the King.' Taunting him, they stripped the King's Herald of the servant's coat, which the Bishop had given him, and threw Francis, naked once again, into a ditch."

"No way! God could not possibly let such a day end like that!"

"Ironic, isn't it? If Francis needed positive reinforcement from God that he had done the right thing, he didn't get it."

Spiritual Practice 1
Receiving Christ into the Soul

LIKE MANY OF US, in the midst of a sometimes good life of partying and a sometimes sad life of feeling purposeless, Francis, in a random moment, suddenly experienced Jesus touching his heart, "filling it with such surpassing sweetness that he could neither speak nor move."[1] As this sweetness took over his life, he began to withdraw from the "tumult of earthly things and applied himself secretly to receive Jesus Christ into his soul with that pearl of great price[2] which he so desired as to be willing to sell all he possessed in order to gain it."[3]

When this happened to Francis, he began to withdraw in secret to pray, while at the same time, finding ways to serve God—from giving his money generously where it was needed to personally laboring to help those in need.

STEP 1

Find a secret place to pray. Find a place where there is nothing to distract you from God. Francis liked to pray in a cave.

---

1. Brother Leo. *Legend of the Three Companions – Life of St. Francis of Assisi*. Kindle location 117.

2. Jesus said, "The kingdom of heaven is like a merchant in search of fine pearls; on finding one pearl of great value, he went and sold all that he had and bought it." Matt 13:45–46.

3. Brother Leo. *Legend of the Three Companions – Life of St. Francis of Assisi*. Kindle location 126.

Step 2

Apply yourself to receiving Jesus into your soul. We all have things that keep us from wanting to give our entire self and life to God. Ask God to show you what these things are and how to keep them from being obstacles. Meditate on this in your secret place of prayer.

Step 3

Act. The presence of Jesus in our lives always leads us to action, just as it did for Francis. Ask the Holy Spirit to show you what action God is calling you to take. Meditate on this and journal your thoughts.

PART 2

The Way Lost

4

Crisis in the Community
Galatians 1:6–10

SLEEP CAME EASILY ON the eve of St. Francis's Feast Day. We slept with our windows open and when we awoke early the next morning, two doves, one white and one gray, were sitting on the sill watching us. The weather could not have been more perfect. At 8:30 that morning authorities and delegates from all over Italy would gather in the Piazza del Comune, the huge Assisi square, to recommit themselves in honor of Francis to the *Pace Civile,* or Civil Peace.

The *Pace Civile* was a document that put an end to civil unrest in Assisi. Years before the Franciscan Order was formed there began a civil disagreement between the common people and the nobility of Assisi. To put it simply, the wealthy had been unwilling to share their power and wealth with the poor. By 1210, tensions spiraled out of control between the two factions. Francis, determined to negotiate peace, took up the cause of the common people. He negotiated the *Pace Civile* in which the nobility renounced all feudal rights in consideration of a small periodic payment. In addition, the common people were no longer taxed unjustly and exiles were allowed to return in peace. Notably, the document opened with an appeal to the Holy Spirit to guide Assisi. Francis had proven himself a friend of the poor, a leader willing to get involved in the governing of Assisi, and a wise negotiator.[1]

---

1. Sabatier, *The Road to Assisi,* 59 60.

I was an early riser, unlike my softly snoring husband, and had several free hours before we needed to make our way to the Piazza del Comune. So I went to the common area of the bed and breakfast where there was a massive dining room table where I could work.

I had been pondering the crisis that was consuming Paul's community in Galatia. Some unnamed Jewish Christian leaders had shown up after Paul had established his community. Paul had already moved on to create another Christian community in a different region when he heard about what was going on. This epistle was his desperate attempt to try to stop the damage that was being done.

I am astonished that you are so quickly deserting the one who called you in the grace of Christ and are turning to a different gospel—not that there is another gospel, but there are some who are confusing you and want to pervert the gospel of Christ.[2] But even if we or an angel from heaven should proclaim to you a gospel contrary to what we proclaimed to you, let that one be accursed![3] As we have said before, so now I repeat, if anyone proclaims to you a gospel contrary to what you received, let that one be accursed! Am I now seeking human approval, or God's approval? Or am I trying to please people? If I were still pleasing people, I would not be a servant of Christ.[4] (Gal 1:6–10)

Paul had been teaching that the Christian life (including his own) was made possible because of God's grace—the gift of being acceptable to God even

---

2. The word translated pervert means to misrepresent or turn away.

3. Accursed is a translation of the Greek word *anathema*. In the first century, *anathema* meant "dedicated to a deity," but since then has come to mean "accursed." Paul was using it to say, "Let that one be dedicated (or re-dedicated) to God." It is an appeal for the person to reconsider the position they are taking and to realign themselves with God. However, many scholars have understood Paul to be placing a curse on these people with whom he disagrees. Luther is one such scholar, "Here riseth a question, whether it be lawful for a Christian to curse? . . . Why not? Howbeit not always, nor for every cause" (Luther, *Galatians*, 479). Luther, during his ministry, used this Greek word, *anathema*, to curse everyone he disagreed with from the peasants to the Jews. Jesus, however, taught differently: "Do not judge, so that you may not be judged. For with the judgment you make you will be judged, and the measure you give will be the measure you get" (Mat 7:1–2). It is never right for a Christian to wish harm on others. Pray that others will receive grace instead.

4. The word that is translated servant is the Greek word *doulos* and literally means slave. Paul was emphasizing that his voluntary commitment to follow Christ was strong and permanent.

though we have not earned and do not deserve it. On our behalf, Christ both earned and deserved God's acceptance. Because of Christ, God's gift of acceptance belongs to us without condition. Furthermore, Paul believed one not only came into relationship with Jesus through grace, but one also lived the Christian life through grace.

On the other hand, these Jewish Christian leaders taught the Christian life was to be a constant struggle to become acceptable to God. They believed that after one was a follower of Jesus, then God's continual acceptance was to be achieved by becoming holy. Holiness, to them, meant doing a variety of things such as believing a right theology, doing a set of good works, and following a right list of rules. In Galatia, the Jewish Christian leaders were focused on the law. They were teaching the Galatians that to get on this path to achieve holiness they must first become Jewish and agree to follow the Jewish law. Of course, this would require that the men be circumcised, since that was how one was initiated into the Jewish faith and how the commitment was made to follow the Jewish law.

As the sun rose higher and higher over the holy city of Assisi, it occurred to me that Francis was in much the same boat as these Jewish Christians. He too believed the Christian life was a constant struggle to be acceptable to God. Admirably, his striving to obtain acceptance was not based on fear, but on his deep love for God. Yet, instead of following the Jewish law, he focused himself on adherence to the instructions of Jesus to the apostles.[5] Those were the instructions Jesus had spoken through a priest to Francis that day in the Chiesa di Santa Maria degli Angeli. For Francis these verses boiled down to evangelizing and serving others while giving up material things and the desires of the flesh. Even on his deathbed, he asked the friars, "When I am dying, lay me naked on the ground . . . and let me lie there after I am dead for the length of time it takes to walk one mile unhurriedly." He wished to die owning nothing—not even a set of clothes—so that God would be pleased with him.[6]

For Paul, this was not a minor theological issue. Struggling to *earn* God's acceptance—by any means—was a rejection of God's grace. It put roadblocks in the way of hearing the Spirit's voice, which wanted to guide Jesus's followers to do the will of God. It was the difference between a life lived in relationship with and obedience to the Spirit and a life of obedience to a long list of rules. The Spirit loved, nurtured, comforted, and directed

5. Matt 10:5–15.
6. Celano, *The Francis Trilogy*, 306.

the Galatians in all kinds of situations. The law would judge and enslave them, never able to love them or understand the nuances of their lives.

Therefore, Paul was passionate about fixing this situation—calling the Galatians back to a life lived in grace. He believed that if he failed, the Galatians would never have the lives they could have had. They would be enslaved to a set of rules. The vitality of their spirits would be imprisoned. Their lives would become a distorted version of what a Christian's life should be. Christ would become unrecognizable within them.

Paul had personally experienced what life was like living under Jewish rules and customs. It was his way of life—a lifestyle that led Paul to believe incorrect things about God. So much so that he thought persecuting Christians was the will of God. He had been so faithful to these rules and to the leaders who taught them that he participated in the stoning death of a young follower of Jesus named Stephen.[7] Then Paul met Christ. Christ set Paul free from his rule following and people pleasing: "Am I now seeking human approval, or God's approval? Or am I trying to please people? If I were still pleasing people, I would not be a servant of Christ."[8]

Sitting at that massive table staring at these verses, something else occurred to me—something contradictory. Paul, who was so adamant that the true gospel would set us free, also called himself a "slave of Christ."[9] He had been set free *from* religion and religious rules *to* become a slave of Christ. He had voluntarily given himself up to be the hands and feet of Christ. Despite their disagreements, Paul and Francis had this in common. Francis had been set free *from* materialism *to* become the slave of Christ too.

"What ya doin?" asked my husband, breaking the silence and startling me on purpose. I glared, then smiled at him as he kissed me on the back of my neck. Just then, the owner of the bed and breakfast entered the main door from the street, arriving to set out *prima colazione*, or breakfast, for us. Irresistible *fette biscottates*, *caffe lattes*, and a variety of fresh breads and sweet jams were set on the table. The intermingling aroma was intoxicating. I picked up my laptop to get it out of the way. After chatting with the owner and sampling one of everything, with a latte in hand, my husband and I walked up three floors back to our room so I could shower.

---

7. Acts 6:1—8:3.

8. Gal 1:10.

9. Gal 1:10, Rom 1:1, Eph 3:7, Phil 1:1, Col 1:7, and Titus 1:1.

My patient husband leaned against the bathroom sink and listened to my musings on Paul. I summarized by saying Paul believed the Christian life was lived by jettisoning the rules and obeying the Spirit. The Jewish Christians believed the Christian life was lived by following the Jewish rules. Francis believed the Christian life was lived by following a new set of rules, which he thought Jesus had given him.

My husband handed me a towel and I dressed so we could scurry to the main *piazza* in Assisi, each with our own little point-and-shoot camera dangling around our neck. Enthusiastic festival hosts ushered us to the parade route up Corso Giuseppe Mazzini toward the Piazza del Comune. Little did we know, but likely because my husband's Italian wasn't as fluent as he hoped, we had misunderstood and ended up grouped with the *paparazzi* outside the Palazzo dei Priori, or the town hall. Inside, dignitaries, including the prime minister, were gathering to renew the *Pace Civile* and line up for the parade. The proper *paparazzi* had credentials hanging around their necks, assistants with clipboards taking notes, and expensive cameras in their hands. Yet no one said anything to us. Professional men and women of the *polizia,* dressed in their finest uniforms carrying colorful banners representing their *comune,* stood in place chatting cheerfully.[10] Meanwhile *sindaci,* or city mayors, from across the region were inside. A massive door, with a smaller door cut into it for daily use, was fully opened, revealing stairs to the room where the signing of the *Pace Civile* was taking place. Above the door flew the flags of Italy and Assisi. Big wrought iron lanterns, held up by wrought iron lions, were mounted on the walls. The atmosphere in the piazza was nothing if not playful.

Close to us, a group of distinguished grey haired men dressed in long light grey robes with gold trim huddled together smiling and gossiping. My husband pointed to their banner: "*Compagnia dei Cavalieri—Assisi.*"[11]

"Those are the Knights of Assisi?" I surmised.

"Either that or they stole their banner," he chuckled.

"Are you thinking what I'm thinking?" I turned to look at him astonished. There must be a good explanation, but I didn't know what it was. The men we saw on the Satriano ride were young and they looked sturdy like one might suppose the Knights of Assisi would look. These guys, although each remarkably good looking, retired ten years back and I'd wager none of them have been on a two-day long horse ride in a while!

10. See picture 17 in the appendix.

11. See picture 18 in the appendix.

"No, I'm not thinking that!" He teased me. "You were going to say maybe the hostess at the *agriturismo* was right and we had fallen under some sort of Giovanni spell that afternoon in Satriano."

"Maybe."

"Well, those guys are obviously not the men we saw on horseback riding through Satriano a month ago, but Giovanni is no ghost!"

"I know, but it is a mystery!" I wanted him to play along.

Before my husband could make fun of me further, the top dignitaries of Italy, including the prime minister, exited city hall just feet from us. A few unarmed *polizia*, walking with the Prime Minster, lined up behind men who were wearing plumed blue velvet hats and medieval costumes.[12] The bells in the Torre del Popolo tower rang joyfully for several minutes summoning all of Assisi to the celebration.[13] Then, on cue, several of the costumed men lifted horns, with red flags hanging from the horns' long pipes, toward the sky. With exuberant fanfare, they blasted the horns, announcing the beginning of the procession. Other costumed men held pole-arms—wooden poles with sharp pointed metal spikes. A few jesters were wandering around and about the crowd creating merriment. The *paparazzi* snapped pictures and we followed suit. As the *paparazzi* moved with the parade, we went along with them. No one corrected us. We even returned waves with the people lining the narrow streets who parted to make way for the dignitaries and those like us who were now part of the procession.

"Where are we going?" yelled my husband over the noise.

"To the Basilica of St. Francis for Mass," I yelled back. When the noise stilled a bit, I added, "Except Mass is by invitation only. So unless you have an invitation, we get to wait outside."

As we approached the basilica, a man was ushering the *paparazzi* to the lower level courtyard.[14] They were forbidden to photograph Mass and this way they could get in place for the prime minister's speech that would take place afterwards. This usher was the first to recognize we didn't belong and pointed us toward the upper courtyard where the dignitaries had marched past. They were entering the upper basilica as their assistants produced their invitations. Behind them was a procession of Franciscan monks. We had run out of luck so we walked over to the south courtyard wall and leaned on it.

12. See picture 19 in the appendix.

13. See picture 20 in the appendix.

14. See picture 21 in the appendix.

"That was fun!" I declared as I closed my eyes and turned my face toward the sun, soaking up the rays. It was a cloudless day. The courtyard was filling up now with others who had fallen in line with the parade as it passed them.

"It *was* fun!" came a joyful voice. I turned. Giovanni was leaning on the wall next to me swinging his bare foot with his ragged tunic fluttering a bit in the constant breeze that floated over the upper basilica courtyard. It was the first time I had noticed that his feet were red and swollen with little white spots all over his naked ankles.

"Giovanni! I've been wanting to talk to you! And here you are!" I smiled ear-to-ear just because he was smiling.

"Here I am, indeed!"

Overcoming my regard for his privacy, I blurted out, "Giovanni, why don't you have shoes? The ground is too cold to go barefoot any longer this season."

"That's what you wanted to talk to me about young lady?" he teased.

"Not exactly."

He answered my question simply and with an air of seriousness, "My aim is to be authentic to Francis's teachings in order to remind the brothers of who their father was." Then he elaborated, "I want to set a contrast between the myth Francis has become and his unquenchable desire to serve God. Like you said of both Paul and Francis, so much of who they were and what they taught has been distorted into something easier for the rest of us to live with. Even we Franciscans have distorted it with our fancy brown tunics and leather shoes."

He looked around the upper basilica courtyard. "Yet, Francis would have loved this," he nodded toward the merriment in the courtyard. It was filled with people of all ages and nationalities who had come to celebrate St. Francis's Feast Day—young parents and adoring grandparents sitting together in the grass doting on their *bambini*. "Francis would have loved that his life was an excuse for people to gather under Brother Sun and warm their souls. Nothing would've pleased him more."

As he talked, I looked past him to see two delightful middle-aged Franciscan nuns.[15] They were adorned with crinkly laugh lines around their sparkling eyes, dressed in their white habits and black veils, and seated a few

15. Over the centuries, several orders for women with the Franciscan name have formed separately from the order of Saint Clare. They are all devoted followers of St Francis.

feet down from Giovanni on the wall. The plumper of the two had gelato in a cone and was really enjoying it despite the fact it wasn't even lunchtime yet.[16] The two of them perfectly personified all the charm of Assisi.

"But look at that basilica," Giovanni motioned toward the pink-beige exterior. "Francis would never have wanted that. His dead body lies in a tomb in the lower level on a bed that's a million times fancier than any bed he would've ever slept in. He would've far preferred the money be spent to enhance the lives of the living."

"Giovanni, how'd it happen that Francis's vision was distorted even by those who'd taken vows in his order?"

Giovanni stood in order to move around me to shake my husband's hand. My husband had been distracted documenting the celebration with hundreds of photographs. His theory was if he took enough pictures, a few of them would be worth keeping. In fact, I guess that was a theory to which we both subscribed given the number of photographs we took home. As Giovanni shook my husband's hand, we all turned to look over the wall past the paved lower courtyard and into the valley beyond. Far below us stood the Basilica di Santa Maria degli Angeli.[17] Giovanni pointed toward it and said, "That is where the distortion began."

"At his death in the Transito?" The Transito was the small stone building used as an infirmary by the Franciscans where Francis transitioned from this life into the next. It was now housed within the Basilica di Santa Maria degli Angeli along with the Porziuncola chapel.

"No, before that. This story happened between the time Francis's men had been incorporated into the church—accepted as an official order—and his death."

Giovanni went on to explain that where the basilica now sits the Franciscans were given the *piccola porzione,* or small portion of land, appropriately known today as the Porziuncola. There the brothers built small huts of interlaced tree branches, straw, and mud. The tiny huts provided some, but barely any, shelter. In time, they enclosed the primitive village with a hedge. Thus was born the thirteenth century Franciscan headquarters.

As the Franciscan Order quickly grew, it became large enough to require organized leadership. This was something Francis wasn't skilled in doing. He could provide spiritual leadership and inspiration in spades, but practical day-to-day leadership was not his forte. Nor was he concerned

16. See picture 22 in the appendix.

17. See picture 23 in the appendix.

about the strain his growing fraternity put on the townspeople who were called upon to provide food as the men begged for alms at each meal. In short, Francis was not concerned about everyday matters. His faith was strong that God would provide.

However, the church, specifically Cardinal Ugolino, who was responsible for the order and who would later become Pope Gregory IX, was very concerned. In addition, there were dissenters within the Franciscans themselves who questioned whether the poverty they had originally pledged themselves to was practical. Would a coat and shoes in winter have hurt them? Would providing for their own food have been wrong? Would allowing for their theological education have been detrimental? These were all things Francis forbade his men to have and do.

The cardinal approached Francis with these concerns. In fact, both Cardinal Ugolino and Dominic, the father of the Dominican Order, came together for a visit to the Porziuncola. Ugolino hoped to join the two orders into one. Dominic was a practical leader with a well-organized, but as of yet, small order. Francis was an impractical leader with a big disorganized order. United, Ugolino hoped they would become stronger. Francis, however, was flatly unwilling to even discuss the possibility with the cardinal. Instead, he called the brothers together and in front of the cardinal stated that of all the Holy Orders, the Franciscans alone were practicing the truth, thus passionately dissing all other orders—not just the Dominicans.

Giovanni put his hand on his hips and almost whispered as if it was shameful, "In that public forum, Francis told Ugolino . . ." Giovanni paused, then raising his voice imitating Francis, "Don't you come around here speaking to me about how the Dominicans or other orders are living, because God gave us—not the other orders—the truth! God is going to use the Franciscans to 'make a new covenant with the world!'"[18]

With that, Ugolino decided to leave Francis alone. Francis, firmly grounded in his own convictions, had shown he was unwilling to learn from others or take the advice of church leaders. Dominic, on the other hand, often sought and took advice from others. This visit with Francis was no different. Dominic was deeply influenced during that visit by the lifestyle practiced by the Franciscans living at the Porziuncola. He was impressed by how rejecting materialism freed the Franciscans to concentrate on the work of God. He learned from the Franciscans and shortly afterwards began to incorporate the lessons he learned into the Dominican way.

18. Sabatier, *The Road to Assisi*, 98.

Dominic was open to learning from others. Francis was not. In the years that followed, Dominic would continue to grow a robust order, while the Franciscans would be described as "the most tempest-tossed society the world has ever known."[19]

Although Dominic embraced the poverty Francis taught, there was a difference theologically in how the two men saw poverty's relationship to the Christian life. Francis believed keeping the rule of poverty—giving up all one had—was the ultimate expression of the Christian life. It had set him free. For Dominic, poverty was not a requirement of the Christian life, but a tool—one of many tools—that might be used to do the work of God.

"This meeting between the cardinal, Dominic, and Francis was the beginning of the end," said Giovanni sadly. "Francis did not understand what it took to lead. To top it off, instead of staying around to lead his order, he went off on a mission to Syria and the Holy Land in hopes of converting the Muslims who occupied the land. He had such a big heart. He believed if the Muslims were converted to Christianity, then it would be an end of the violent crusades. Alternatively, if he were martyred in his attempt to convert the Muslims, he believed he would have given the ultimate to Christ. Either way, Francis believed it would be a spiritual success. However, back at home while he was away, those he had left in charge were busy lessening the vow of poverty. When he did not return in the time planned, Francis was even reported dead."

"Falsely, of course." my husband mused.

"Yes, falsely," smiled Giovanni. "He was very much alive, but forever cut off at the knees by those who were taking charge of his order during his absence. They began making changes."

"What kind of changes?" I asked.

"They began providing for the men's physical needs—food, housing, more substantial clothing. For spiritual needs too—books and theological education. However, upon Francis's return, he was devastated. In the weeks and months following, he would write to the brothers, 'From here forward, I am dead to you.'[20] And thus Francis, seeing he could not stay as their leader, stepped down. He had intended to stay in the order as their brother under a new leader, but it became a very difficult struggle as changes within the order began to take place."

---

19. Sabatier, *The Road to Assisi*, 99.

20. Sabatier, *The Road to Assisi*, 111.

"So Francis just walked away from his order?" asked my husband astonished.

"Not exactly," answered Giovanni. "He was never far away. Even on his deathbed, he was still grieving. He would wake suddenly from fever and cry out, 'Where are they who have stolen my family?' He talked of 'creating a new family' who would return to the original Franciscan rule of life. He wrote letters to his order and to all Christians, which emphasized the folly of those who set their hearts on the possession of earthly goods."[21]

"How very thought-provoking," I pondered. "The communities of both Francis and Paul dived into crisis mode not too terribly long after they were founded. Both crises occurred while the leaders were away. The Franciscans entered into crisis over the rule of poverty, adherence to which was key to Francis's understanding of how to live the Christian life. The Galatians entered into crisis over religious rules—the rejection of which was key to how Paul believed the Christian life should be lived."

The three of us were still staring down into the valley when we heard a commotion behind us. Mass was letting out and people were filing down to the lower basilica courtyard where the prime minister of Italy would be speaking. Giovanni excused himself saying he would find us later. We watched him enter a small, insignificant arched door towards the *sacro convento*, the Friary of Saint Francis.

"I guess he lives there?" my husband asked.

"I don't know. I think it's a seminary now."

We both stared after him until it was obvious our question would go unanswered. Then my husband asked, "So, how *do* we live the Christian life?"

"You really want to strip to your skivvies in front of town hall, don't you?" I teased again.

"Only if you go first." Then seriously, he went on, "Paul rejected religion and its rules. Francis rejected materialism and instituted a list of rules. And both of their communities struggled with following their leader's vision for the Christian life."

My husband and I had started walking back through town leaving the crowd behind. I certainly didn't speak enough Italian to understand what the prime minister would say in his speech and my husband would only understand the slowly spoken words so we decided not to stay. Plus we wanted to take advantage of seeing what we hoped would be an empty San

---

21. Sabatier, *The Road to Assisi*, 146–150.

Damiano just outside the Assisi gates at the other end of town. This was the church where Francis had first heard Jesus speak to him.

5

Revelation

Galatians 1:11–24

GOING THE OPPOSITE DIRECTION of the pedestrian traffic, which was headed to see the prime minister, we headed east, back across Assisi, and exited the city walls at Porta Nuova—the *new* gate in the city walls. We laughed about how long the people of Assisi had been calling this old gate new. The city had expanded its walls in the fourteenth century so we figured 700 years was a good rough estimate. The gate had inscribed upon it Francis's final blessing on the city:

> May the Lord bless you, Holy City Faithful to God
> Because through you many souls shall be saved
> And in you many servants of the Most High will dwell
> And from you many shall be chosen for the eternal kingdom.

We walked down a long steep cobblestone slope toward the valley. In Francis's day, the Chiesa di San Damiano, although just a mile from the walls of Assisi, was unprotected and isolated. Francis would have walked to the chapel through terraced groves of olive trees. We took it all in, admiring the cypress trees planted on one side while shorter fragrant lavender and rosemary bushes covered the other side, opening to a stunning view of Assisi above and the Valle Umbra below.

About halfway down the hill, the path ended and we came upon San Damiano.[1] The stone building itself had an interesting history dating back

1. See picture 25 in the appendix.

to the eleventh century. From an architectural perspective, it was now the victim of many renovations and additions. Its façade had windows—some square, some round, some rectangular—placed randomly. Upper floor doors opened into thin air. Two Franciscans stood under the porch whispering to each other next to a sign that once again said *silenzio*. They smiled as we passed them to enter the building.

The chapel was small, dark, and simple. It glowed a golden color with floor tiles in shades of muted reds, oranges, and creams. Dominating the room was a flat Byzantine crucifix with the image of Jesus painted on it.[2] The dark red and black background was in stark contrast to the bright body of Jesus. Notably, this icon did not depict Christ in agony. Instead, Jesus looked upon us with dark welcoming eyes and arms outstretched as if wanting to embrace us. It immediately made me feel welcome. Other witnesses to the crucifixion—the three Marys, John, and a centurion—were also painted on the cross, but in a smaller size, which made them appear to be standing in the background. The six patrons of Assisi—Damian, Michael, Rufino, John the Baptist, Peter, and Paul—were also present, as were angels and some Bible characters. At the top, beneath the disembodied hand of God, was an image of Jesus joyfully exiting the tomb.

"That is a replica of the cross that spoke to Francis," I whispered to my husband.

"What happened to the original?" he whispered back.[3]

To this the monks, who had slipped in unbeknownst to us, whispered, "*Per favore, silenzio!*"

"But we are the only ones here!" my husband mouthed to me as he looked around the chapel.

"Shhh!" I mouthed back trying not to encourage him. We entered one of the two-person pews and knelt, studying the cross and praying the same prayer, asking the same question we had prayed in every church and chapel along the Cammino di Assisi, "How do we live the Christian life?"

At twenty-two years of age, Francis, the philanderer and rabble-rouser, had fallen into a state of discontentment. Doctors today might have diagnosed him with post-traumatic stress disorder or simply depression.[4]

---

2. See picture 26 in the appendix.

3. Today the original cross hangs in the Basilica of St. Clare. San Damiano functioned as a primitive convent for the Poor Clares until 1253, when Clare died. For their protection, the sisters moved the convent to where the Basilica of St. Clare now stands and brought the cross with them.

4. After using this story of Francis as an example in a sermon, I was approached by

A few years earlier, he had followed his friends and townsmen into battle against the neighboring village of Perugia where he was promptly captured and held prisoner for about a year while his captors demanded a ransom. There his fellow prisoners often speculated whether he had gone mad because of his strange but consistent lightness of heart. Perhaps he was in denial. He spent his days in captivity planning great adventures and telling the other captives that one day he would be adored by all of the world. However, upon returning home and falling back into his old playboy lifestyle, he became gravely ill and sunk into despair. When his health started to recover, he began to wander the countryside alone looking for meaning.

One day Francis wandered into San Damiano to pray. At that time, it was in disrepair and abandoned by all but one poor priest who barely had the funds to feed himself, much less take care of the building and grounds. In the sparse, dark church hung the Byzantine crucifix. Francis knelt before it and prayed:

> Most High and glorious God, enlighten the darkness of my heart and give me truer faith, more certain hope, and perfect charity, sense and knowledge of you, so that I may carry out your holy and true command for my life."[5]

As Francis prayed, the image of Christ took on life and spoke into the very depths of his heart. It was then he knew Jesus accepted his oblation and desired all of his being. This was a moment of transformation for Francis: "For the first time, no doubt, Francis had been brought into direct, personal, and intimate contact with Jesus Christ."[6]

Specifically, Francis heard the tender and compassionate voice of Christ say, "Francis, do you not see that my house is falling into ruin? Go, and repair it for me."[7] At first, he understood the command to mean he must repair the run-down San Damiano. Then later, he expanded his call to the dilapidated small rural churches dotting the countryside. However, as more time went by, he realized Christ had not just been speaking of the

---

a female psychiatrist. She told me that she believed that Francis was mentally ill and went on to give a professional diagnosis. That took me by surprise. I wondered aloud if that didn't negate his spirituality and ministry. Her response delighted me, "Absolutely not! His life can be an inspiration to those with mental illnesses! They too can influence the entire world for good."

5. Sweeney, *The St. Francis Prayer Book*, 121.

6. Sabatier, *The Road to Assisi*, 35–36.

7. Brother Leo, *Legend of the Three Companions*, Chapter 5, Kindle location 199.

physical church buildings, but also of the spiritual church—"the Church which Christ had acquired with His own blood."[8] Francis was neither a priest nor seminarian—in fact, he had no authority whatsoever in the church. However, in the end Francis would come to believe that Jesus had given him the important directive to rebuild the spiritual church.

After soaking in the quietness of the chapel, my husband and I found our way into the interior courtyard. It was such a contrast from the darkness of the church. Summer flowers—more red geraniums like those we had seen at Eremo delle Carceri—bloomed brilliantly inside the protective walls. We sat down on one of the low stone borders surrounding four meticulously maintained beds of ornamental grass.

"So Jesus gave Francis his life mission in that chapel," said my husband. "Looks like if God can make a cross talk, then God could at least send us an email!"

"That would be nice, but you know it wasn't rose petals and sunshine from there on and forever more for Francis. At first no one—including the poor priest assigned here—believed Francis."

"Really? They had problems with a talking cross?"

"No. It wasn't the talking cross the priest questioned. The priest had recently seen Francis cavorting with his friends and thought a joke was being played on him.[9] By the way, did you see the niche by the main door? In Francis's day, it was a small window."[10]

"Yes. I saw the *finestra dei soldi!*" my husband said with that perfect Italian accent. "The window of the money?"

"Yes. Shortly after Francis's encounter with Jesus, he loaded up his father's inventory of fabric onto his horse and took it to the neighboring city of Foligno where he sold everything."

"I remember this story. You told me that day in front of the fountain of Piazza del Vescovado."

"Exactly. Well, he not only sold his dad's inventory in Foligno, but he sold the horse he rode in on! He had to walk back to San Damiano, but in his pockets, he was carrying a rather large offering."

"I bet the priest was glad to get it."

"No, the priest wouldn't take Francis's money. He was too afraid of Pietro Bernardone. The *finestra dei soldi* was where Francis threw the rejected

8. Celano, *The Francis Trilogy*, 168.

9. Brother Leo, *Legend of the Three Companions*, 221.

10. See picture 27 in the appendix.

offering. And let me tell you, it was a darn good thing for the priest he didn't accept it. Soon enough Pietro showed up at San Damiano full of rage. Fortunately, the priest had not been without compassion toward Francis and had hidden him away from his father. As Francis hid, he spent days crying—begging God to show him his next steps, while at the same time rejoicing that Christ had given him good work to do."

"Francis's first encounter with Jesus was dramatic and colorful. It suited him."

"Yes, but it's also interesting to note he'd been around the church since birth. He wasn't new to Jesus or Christianity. He'd been baptized in the Roman Catholic Church as an infant and had gone to the best Catholic school in town.[11] No doubt, he and his family attended church—at least on all the holy days—and contributed to the parish."

"Even so, this revelation seems to be his first real encounter with Christ."

I had gotten into the habit of comparing Francis to Paul so as we sat in the courtyard, I went down that path again.

For I want you to know, brothers and sisters, that the gospel that was proclaimed by me is not of human origin; for I did not receive it from a human source, nor was I taught it, but I received it through a revelation of Jesus Christ.[12] You have heard, no doubt, of my earlier life in Judaism. I was violently persecuting the church of God and was trying to destroy it. I advanced in Judaism beyond many among my people of the same age, for I was far more zealous for the traditions of my ancestors. But when God, who had set me apart before I was born[13] and called me through his grace, was pleased to reveal his Son to me[14], so that I might proclaim him among the Gentiles, I did not confer with any human being, nor did I go up to Jerusalem

---

11. Francis was baptized in the Cathedral of San Rufino and his school was located in what is now the Basilica of St. Clare.

12. The phrase "revelation of Jesus Christ" is better understood as the "unveiling of Jesus Christ." For Paul, it was not a piece of theology that was revealed to him, it was Jesus himself. Wright, *Paul for Everyone: Galatians*, 6.

13. "Before I was born" is literally "in my mother's womb." I like the literal translation best, because it honors the uteruses of women as a holy place where God is at work.

14. God "was pleased to reveal his Son *to* me" is unique to the NRSV translation. I think the more common translation is better: God "was pleased to reveal his Son *in* me." Paul writes later, "It is no longer I who live, but Christ who lives in me" (Gal 2:20). This indwelling of God is a very important part of Paul's gospel.

> *to those who were already apostles*[15] *before me, but I went away at*
> *once into Arabia, and afterwards I returned to Damascus. Then after*
> *three years I did go up to Jerusalem to visit Cephas and stayed with*
> *him fifteen days; but I did not see any other apostle except James the*
> *Lord's brother. In what I am writing to you, before God, I do not lie!*
> *Then I went into the regions of Syria and Cilicia,*[16] *and I was still*
> *unknown by sight to the churches of Judea that are in Christ; they*
> *only heard it said, "The one who formerly was persecuting us is now*
> *proclaiming the faith he once tried to destroy." And they glorified*
> *God because of me.*[17] *(Gal 1:11–24)*

Paul also had a dramatic first encounter with Jesus. His story is told in Acts 9. Here he goes by the name of Saul.[18]

> Meanwhile Saul, still breathing threats and murder against the
> disciples of the Lord, went to the high priest and asked him for
> letters to the synagogues at Damascus, so that if he found any
> who belonged to the Way,[19] men or women, he might bring them
> bound to Jerusalem. Now as he was going along and approaching
> Damascus, suddenly a light from heaven flashed around him. He
> fell to the ground and heard a voice saying to him, "Saul, Saul, why
> do you persecute me?" He asked, "Who are you, Lord?" The reply
> came, "I am Jesus, whom you are persecuting. But get up and enter
> the city, and you will be told what you are to do." The men who
> were traveling with him stood speechless because they heard the
> voice but saw no one. Saul got up from the ground, and though his

15. Apostle has come to mean an official position in the church, but it literally means messenger or envoy. Paul is using the description not the title. We have no evidence that Paul was ever given any official title or ordination by the church.

16. Syria refers to the area south of Tarsus around Antioch. Cilicia is the area around Tarsus—Paul's hometown. Betz, *Galatians*, 80.

17. The Judean churches were the oldest churches. They were Jewish Christians, who kept the laws of the Old Testament. Paul likely mentioned them here to say that these churches once approved of him based on his conversion, but would no longer approve of him based on his theology, which he described in Galatians. Betz, *Galatians*, 80.

18. As mentioned in Acts 13:9, Paul and Saul were interchangeable names for the apostle. Saul was his Jewish name and Paul was his Roman name (taken as a Roman citizen), which he likely used as he ventured into gentile territory in order to make the gentiles he encountered more comfortable with him.

19. The Way was what the Jesus movement was first called when it was still part of the Jewish faith. Jesus was a Jew, his first disciples were Jewish, and Christianity was originally viewed by both Jewish Christians and Jews as one of the many tolerated sects within the Jewish faith. It was not until Paul and others began persecuting Jewish Christians that Christianity moved out of the synagogues and temples into secret house churches.

eyes were open, he could see nothing; so they led him by the hand and brought him into Damascus. For three days he was without sight, and neither ate nor drank. (Act 9:1–9)

For Paul and Francis both, their first encounters with Jesus took place without the guidance, direction, or blessing of anyone in authority within the church. God called them directly, apart from and outside of the existing church. Both saw and heard Jesus speak to them directly. Both were given a mission in which their lives would never be normal again. Paul's mission is found in Acts:

> Now there was a disciple in Damascus named Ananias. The Lord said to him in a vision, "Ananias." He answered, "Here I am, Lord." The Lord said to him, "Get up and go to the street called Straight, and at the house of Judas[20] look for a man of Tarsus named Saul. At this moment he is praying, and he has seen in a vision a man named Ananias come in and lay his hands on him so that he might regain his sight." But Ananias answered, "Lord, I have heard from many about this man, how much evil he has done to your saints in Jerusalem; and here he has authority from the chief priests to bind all who invoke your name." But the Lord said to him, "Go, for he is an instrument whom I have chosen to bring my name before Gentiles and kings and before the people of Israel; I myself will show him how much he must suffer for the sake of my name." So Ananias went and entered the house. He laid his hands on Saul and said, "Brother Saul, the Lord Jesus, who appeared to you on your way here, has sent me so that you may regain your sight and be filled with the Holy Spirit." And immediately something like scales fell from his eyes, and his sight was restored. Then he got up and was baptized. (Acts 9:10–18)

Paul's mission was to spread the news of Jesus to the world—even to the unclean gentiles. But his focus on gentiles and his understanding of the gospel were not readily received among the leaders of the church—even those who had known Jesus personally. Paul, as Jesus had taught and the Old Testament prophet foretold, was learning directly from the Holy Spirit and not the church authorities.[21] Likewise, Francis's mission was to fix the church—a church that didn't recognize his calling, a church that was un-

---

20. This is not the Judas who was a disciple and who betrayed Jesus.

21. Jesus said, "The Holy Spirit . . . will teach you everything" (John 14:26). Jeremiah the prophet wrote, "No longer shall they teach one another, or say to each other, "Know the LORD," for they shall all know me, from the least of them to the greatest" (Jer 31:34).

aware it needed fixing, and a church that didn't welcome him. He too was taught directly by Jesus.

Changing the subject only slightly, I looked around the courtyard and added, "This place is where Clare, the first female follower of Francis, lived cloistered away with the Poor Clares."

"Yesterday on our way into town, I remember seeing the plaque that marked the location of her childhood home. It was next to the Cathedral of San Rufino."

"Yes, she grew up in the wealthy part of town."

"Did she have a revelation too?"

"I'd say it was more like the kind most people have when they decide to follow Jesus."

Clare was sixteen years old, twelve years younger than Francis, when Francis was first invited to preach at the cathedral. His sermons touched her deeply, making her question her family's privilege in a city with deep divisions between the wealthy and the poor. By the time she was eighteen, she had secretly arranged to meet Francis at the little Santa Maria degli Angeli chapel where she would take the vow to conform her life to the same vows the Franciscans had taken. As she arrived in the wooded valley, the Franciscans met her with candles and singing. She took her vows, her hair was tonsured, and she received her veil.[22]

"She too gave up all she had, and this is where she died many years after Francis. It is also where, when Francis was ill, she made him a hut of rat infested reeds to stay in."

"Did she make the hut and invite the rats?"

"No, the rats were unintentional. He was blind by then and they crawled all over him and kept him from resting. He had to be moved because of it."

"I'm speechless," my husband uttered with a look of disgust on his face. "Francis couldn't ever get a break."

"During his stay here was when he wrote the famous Canticle of the Sun[23]. Do you want to see where he wrote it?"

22. Chalippe, *The Life and Legends of Saint Francis of Assisi*, 48–49 .

23. Francis' famous *Canticle of the Sun*, a religious song considered to be the first work of literature written in the Umbrian Italian dialect, has been called many different names over the centuries including *Laudes Creaturarum* (*Praise of the Creatures*), and *Cantico del fratello sole e sorella luna* (*Canticle of Brother Sun and Sister Moon*). In it, Francis praises all of creation and even death. The song was sung by Francis and his closest friends on his deathbed. An English translation of part of the canticle is found in

"A rat infested hut?

"No, the hut is long gone," I said. Pointing to the attached building surrounding the south and east sides of the courtyard, I added, "That is the original convent plus some upgrades."

We went to explore and found a terrace halfway up a set of stairs where Francis is said to have sat in the warm sun of the *giardinetto,* or garden, writing the canticle. We found the Poor Clares' dormitory over the chapel, which had long since been walled in. The Poor Clares had slept there with only a roof over their heads.

"No walls?"

"Nope. Not even in the snow and rain. When they followed Jesus, they too left their old lives of privilege far behind."

"Would we be willing to live the Christian life if it meant leaving our old lives behind?"

The question hung in the air.

this book in Spiritual Practice 4.

6

Rejected Gifts

Galatians 2:1–14

FROM THE SERENITY OF San Damiano, my husband and I decided to return to the Basilica di San Francesco d'Assisi. The morning Mass and speech by the prime minister of Italy were over by now. Our hope was the crowds had dispersed a bit and we could take in the beauty of the basilica's magnificent art and architecture.

As we walked, I explained an event in Paul's life. Sometime after Paul's encounter with Jesus on the road to Damascus, Paul set about telling gentiles about Jesus. For the gentiles whom Paul encountered, it really was good news that God loved them and, through Jesus's death and resurrection, God's grace had set them free.

While Paul was traveling around the eastern world delivering this message, the leaders of the Jesus movement started to get nervous. Paul's ministry had resulted in a large number of gentile converts who were not following Jewish traditions or law. Nor were the male gentiles being circumcised, which was a sign that the men and their families had been initiated into the Jewish faith and had agreed to keep the Jewish religious traditions and the rules of the Torah.[1] Hence, circumcision became the identified problem. The real problem, however, was Jewish nationalism. Simply put, some of the rule following Jewish Christian communities were concerned

---

1. Circumcision was an initiation for adult males, but also for infant boys. Just as the baptized child is initiated into the church today, the circumcised boy was initiated into the Jewish faith based on a commitment made by his parents.

they were losing their heritage, their manner of worship, and their way of life as more and more gentiles entered the Jesus movement.

This all came to a head when a group of "rule followers"[2] from Judea, intent on making the gentiles into proper Torah-keeping Christians, arrived at one of the gentile churches Paul had started in Antioch. There, like in Galatia, these rule followers demanded the gentiles become Jews, meaning the males must be initiated into the faith by being circumcised. A conference in Jerusalem was called and the Antioch church put together a delegation to represent themselves.[3] Paul and Barnabas were the leaders of the delegation.[4] They took along Titus, an uncircumcised gentile Christian, as their living test case. They wanted to introduce him to the church leaders as one who was filled with the Holy Spirit even though he was not circumcised. Their hope was that the leaders would see God had made grace available to an uncircumcised gentile. Paul believed this would put an end to the theology declaring only practicing Jews could be followers of Jesus.

Then after fourteen years I went up again to Jerusalem with Barnabas, taking Titus along with me. I went up in response to a revelation. Then I laid before them (though only in a private meeting with the acknowledged leaders) the gospel that I proclaim among the Gentiles, in order to make sure that I was not running, or had not run, in vain. But even Titus, who was with me, was not compelled to be circumcised, though he was a Greek. But because of false believers secretly brought in, who slipped in to spy on the freedom we have in Christ Jesus, so that they might enslave us—we did not submit to

2. Scholars refer to the Jewish Christians who were causing the problems in Galatia by many different names. Some call them "the circumcision faction," others call them "Judaizers." But as this book will reveal, these names put the focus on the wrong things. First, circumcision was the identified problem, but not the real problem. Second, the real problem was not a Jewish problem, but a religious problem to which no religion—including Christianity—was or is immune. Therefore, the term "rule followers" is used in this book to identify the Christians (who happened to be Jewish) who were equating following Jesus with following a set of religious rules. Many Christians today, the majority of which are gentiles, are rule followers.

3. This conference is commonly known as the "Council of Jerusalem" or the "Apostolic Council." An account of the council is found in Acts 15. It is interesting to note that the account in Acts, written by Luke, differs in some significant ways from the account Paul records in Galatians. These differences will be discussed later.

4. Barnabas had been Paul's mentor, but in Galatians, the sense is that they are colleagues. Barnabas was a Jew from Cyprus who became a Christian while in Jerusalem. Eventually, he would become the church's leader in Antioch.

> *them even for a moment, so that the truth of the gospel might always remain with you.*
>
> *And from those who were supposed to be acknowledged leaders (what they actually were makes no difference to me; God shows no partiality)—those leaders contributed nothing to me. On the contrary, when they saw that I had been entrusted with the gospel for the uncircumcised, just as Peter had been entrusted with the gospel for the circumcised (for he who worked through Peter making him an apostle to the circumcised also worked through me in sending me to the Gentiles), and when James and Cephas and John, who were acknowledged pillars, recognized the grace that had been given to me, they gave to Barnabas and me the right hand of fellowship, agreeing that we should go to the Gentiles and they to the circumcised.[5,6] They asked only one thing, that we remember the poor, which was actually what I was eager to do.*
>
> *But when Cephas came to Antioch, I opposed him to his face, because he stood self-condemned; for until certain people came from James, he used to eat with the Gentiles. But after they came, he drew back and kept himself separate for fear of the circumcision faction. And the other Jews joined him in this hypocrisy, so that even Barnabas was led astray by their hypocrisy. But when I saw that they were not acting consistently with the truth of the gospel, I said to Cephas before them all, "If you, though a Jew, live like a Gentile and not like a Jew, how can you compel the Gentiles to live like Jews?"* (Gal 2:1–14)

Paul was not going to Jerusalem so the Christian leaders could approve his theology. He was confident in what he believed. He was going because he wanted to protect the communities he had started from being misinformed by the wrong theology that the rule followers were teaching.

This translation calls the rule followers "false believers," but that was not exactly what Paul called them. The word translated "false believers" literally means "an untrue friend" and has nothing to do with whether they

---

5. Notice in these verses that both a Peter and a Cephas are mentioned. In Matt 16:18 Jesus renamed Simon giving him a name that meant rock. However, *petros* or Peter means rock in Greek, while *kefa* or Cephas means rock in Aramaic, which is the language Jesus spoke. Most scholars believe that Paul is going back and forth—sometimes calling Simon the name Peter and sometimes calling him the name Cephas. However, there is a possibility that Peter and Cephas are two different people.

6. Notice that the early church divided their ministries not by territories, but by race.

were believers or not. The translators' use of the word "believers" gives the impression Paul was saying the people touting this rule following theology didn't really believe in the death and resurrection of Jesus, which was not true. These rule followers believed in Jesus. They were just mistaken about how to live the Christian life. Paul was not challenging whether the rule followers were believers. Nor was he writing to teach the Galatians how to believe in Jesus. He was writing to the Galatian believers to remind them how to live the Christian life.

There was another often-overlooked point in these verses. To say Titus did not need to become a Jew in order to be a follower of Jesus was not exactly what Paul thought. What Paul believed was far more radical than that. He believed to require anything from Titus in return for God's grace—any human activity at all—was to completely misunderstand the gospel. In other words, Jesus did all the work necessary to reconcile the world to God. The Galatians could do nothing in return. Paul made clear that following any list of religious rules, including the Torah, was the opposite of living the Christian life—the opposite of living under the grace Christ had made possible.

As we walked, a storefront with paintings of busy little monks in a supernatural medieval world caught our eyes. Like busy bees, the little monks were going about daily business in the countryside and town of Assisi. Their world was filled with prayer and work, with nature and companionship. A sign stated it was the work of Norberto Proietti—known simply as Norberto.[7] "Let's go in," I nudged.

The curator of the gallery explained that St. Francis was the artist's moral and intellectual inspiration, stirring him to reject sophisticated artistic techniques for a straightforward style. She said each picture was a depiction of the condition of the soul. If so, the pictures completely captured mine. My favorites were those where some of the monks were floating over fields and through the city. I imagined these flying monks were lost in prayer as they went about their labor.

As we exited the shop and rounded a corner, a woman was on her knees drawing with chalk on the grey stone street.[8] With incredible skill, she had drawn St. Francis, Gandhi, and Mother Teresa. Beneath their faces, she wrote the word, *grazie*, or thank you. She offered boxes of chalk for

---

7. Norberto Proietti (1927–2009) was born in the neighboring city of Spello.

8. See picture 28 in the appendix.

anyone wishing to draw with her. After looking on for a bit, we continued toward the basilica and I continued Paul's story.

In Jerusalem, Paul, Barnabas, and Titus met with the leaders of the church—James, Cephas, and John. According to Paul's account in Galatians, his theology prevailed. Circumcision and a commitment to the Torah would not be a requirement to follow Jesus. According to Paul's account, his theology and ministry were given the blessings of the church leaders. Even Titus, the uncircumcised gentile, was fully accepted by the leaders. The only thing asked of Paul was to remember the poor, which Paul said he was eager to do.[9]

Oddly, this is not exactly the same accounting of the Jerusalem Council given by Luke in Acts 15. On one hand, Luke records the magnificent and life-giving words of Peter, who had been witness to the descending of the Holy Spirit upon the gentile Cornelius:[10]

> And God, who knows the human heart, testified to (the gentiles) by giving them the Holy Spirit, just as he did to us; and in cleansing their hearts by faith he has made no distinction between them and us. Now therefore why are you putting God to the test by placing on the neck of the disciples a yoke that neither our ancestors nor we have been able to bear?[11] We believe that we will be saved through the grace of the Lord Jesus, just as they will. (Acts 15:8–11)

But, on the other hand, in the verses that follow in Acts 15:28–29, Luke also records an edict issued by the Jerusalem Council—a compromise Paul would not have agreed to. This is evidence something went wrong.[12] People walked away from the council with different ideas of what had transpired. According to Luke, the Jerusalem Council issued an edict that, although Christian males would not be required to be circumcised, they would be held to four essential rules from the Torah: do not eat meat sacrificed to idols, do not eat blood, do not eat things that have been strangled, and do not commit sexual immorality.

My parents followed this

9. Titus will become the organizer of the offering to the poor of Jerusalem. In addition, tradition has him ending up as the Bishop of Crete.

10. Acts 10.

11. The yoke Peter is speaking of is the Jewish religious law.

12. Because Paul's and Luke's accounts of the outcome of Apostolic Council differ, some scholars, in order to preserve biblical inerrancy, reason that these were two different councils, but there is no evidence which points to there being two different councils that addressed the same subject matter.

Paul, however, records nothing about this edict nor would he have agreed to even these "essential rules." In fact, we see him take on the first of the essential rules, meat sacrificed to idols, in his letter to the Corinthians. In his first letter to the Corinthians, Paul explains eating meat offered to idols is not wrong in and of itself. He even calls those who refrain from eating the meat sacrificed to idols weak in their faith.[13] But, he also tells those who are eating the meat not to let their freedom become an obstacle to the weak. In other words, he consistently calls on Christians to act in love towards others rather than to live by a list of religious rules.

thinking

Paul would never have agreed to grace plus anything—not even those four essential rules. Paul knew Christ had planned a better way for his followers to live—a life guided by the Spirit. Paul had hoped meeting with the leaders in Jerusalem would settle the whole matter once and for all. Nevertheless, it had not. Not even Cephas and Barnabas stood firm in their convictions.

Not long after the council, Cephas went to Antioch for a visit. There he ate with the "unclean" Christian gentiles—even sharing the Eucharist with them. That was until some people representing James showed up. It was against Jewish law for a Jew to eat with a gentile. We don't know what happened to James, but these Jewish Christians claiming to be his disciples were rule followers. Cephas was afraid he would get in trouble if they saw him eating with uncircumcised gentiles so he stopped eating with them. Paul was enraged by this and called Cephas out for his hypocrisy. Paul was the only one outside of Titus who stood firm in the days following the council.

But things got worse. The next thing Paul knew, these rule followers showed up in Galatia in order to bring this community of gentiles under the religious law and to initiate them into Judaism by circumcising them. Paul was horrified that his community was in danger of being enslaved by the same religious rules Paul himself had been enslaved to all his life. His zeal for religious rules had caused him to participate in the persecution, torture, and death of Christians. Jesus had set Paul free from religious rules and he could not stand the thought of one of his communities being enslaved by them again. For Paul, freedom was not a nice-to-have optional feature of the Christian life, it *was* the Christian life. So Paul would have said the way we live out this freedom cannot be directed by any set of religious rules. We have been set free to be guided by the Holy Spirit.

13. 1 Cor 8:1–10.

69

"How did these different understandings of how to live the Christian life come about?" my husband asked.

The answer was complicated. Both Paul and the early Christian leaders claimed God was on their side. Paul claimed he was taught how to live the Christian life directly by God—not by the disciples or any human being. Likewise, the leaders defended their four essential rules by saying, "it seemed good to the Holy Spirit."[14] Paul stood firm on a "grace alone" theology, whereas the leaders had returned to a "grace plus rules" theology. Adding more complexity to the issue was an inconsistency of which rules should be followed. For some, the list of rules was a commitment to the whole Torah. For others, the list of rules was only the four essentials in the edict issued at the Jerusalem Council. For still others, the list of rules became a list they felt Christ promoted while he was on earth. For Paul, grace was unconditional and did not require any human activity. "Grace plus nothing" was what Paul taught.

"So we are both saved by grace and live the Christian life by grace," I summarized as the Via Frate Elia ended at the basilica.[15]

Platforms erected for the speeches were being systematically dismantled and hauled away in white vans under the direction of a few Franciscans. The lower basilica was once a building that stood on its own, built to house the body of Francis. Strangely, it had been built on what the people of Assisi knew as *collina dell'inferno,* or the hill of hell, where executions had once taken place. Passing through a giant arch, then under a smaller one with a mosaic of Francis's face centered above it, we entered the lower basilica and turned left toward the altar.[16] We walked slowly down the long spacious nave with *cappelle,* or chapels, surrounding the main sanctuary. Although its sparse windows were set off away from the nave, making it dark, it was nonetheless magnificent. Frescos lined every inch of the walls. Halfway down the nave, a set of stairs and a sign pointed downward to the crypt.

At the bottom of the stairs was a tomb, which might have been missed had I not known to look for it. It was actually in the wall behind us. It belonged to Jacopa di Settesoli. She was a close friend of Francis. Having a vision of Francis's approaching death, she made him almond pastries, which he loved, and arranged to bring them to him along with other things for his

14. Acts 15:28.

15. See picture 29 in the appendix.

16. See picture 30 in the appendix.

70

burial. Serendipitously, at the same time, Francis penned her an affection-ate note, which he never sent, because it was revealed to him that she was already on her way bringing him the things he had requested.

> "Dearest, I want you to know that the blessed Lord has done me the grace of revealing that the end of my life is nigh. So, if you want to find me still alive, hurry here to St. Mary of the Angels as soon as you receive this letter, because if you get here later than Saturday, you might not see me alive. And bring with you a hair cloth to wrap my body in, and the candles for the burial. I also ask you to bring me those sweetmeats which you used to give me when I was ill in Rome."[17]

However, when she and her two sons arrived at the *transito,* some of the Franciscans protested her presence because women were forbidden to enter the friary. Francis solved the problem, calling her "Brother Jacopa," pro-claiming her a brother in the Franciscan order.

"Doesn't this just demonstrate that Francis wasn't your usual rule fol-lower?" I asked. "Women weren't allowed to be Franciscans—not allowed in the friary. It was against the rules, but Francis wasn't afraid to break a rule."

"True. I wonder if materialism was just too big a temptation. So much so that he felt he had to formalize it into an unbending rule. Maybe living without possessions was the only way he could personally give his life over to the way of Jesus every day."

"Sure. Perhaps it was what the Holy Spirit had called him to do. But maybe he misunderstood that living in abject poverty wasn't meant for ev-eryone—not even everyone in his order."

"You're saying he took what the Holy Spirit told him to do and spread it too widely to include all others," my husband summarized as other visi-tors came down the stairs to the crypt.

"Too widely and maybe too severely. Giving up all material posses-sions is really not sustainable. But there is so much truth in living simply. What a better place the world would be if wealth was spread widely instead of hoarded."

"It was no secret that church leaders of Francis's day were living in luxury, while there was great need just outside the church doors. True of many church leaders today too."

---

17. Brother Ugolino. *The Little Flowers of St. Francis,* 204–206.

"And churchgoers. Francis's lessons on poverty should not be disregarded."

We stood there a while longer thinking, until we turned and saw that further ahead in the darkness, set off by an iron gate, was the tomb of Francis.

"There is only one thing to say," my husband started then stopped.

"Let me guess—that this is absolutely not what Francis would've wanted?"

"And yet, I think he would've appreciated the art!" my husband laughed. "There were a lot of skilled craftsmen who contributed their best to this building. But on the other hand, this crypt is expensive, dark, and reeks of death and decay, not creation and joy."

We stood there for another moment facing the tomb. Pilgrims waited in a line that circled around the tomb to receive commemorative cards from a monk sitting at a small desk with a basket where one could place an offering. We noticed the pilgrims might write prayer requests on several of the cards and then take them to the tomb where they would place their cards while they spent a moment or two kneeling there and praying. Then they would gather their cards and leave. Right or wrong, this process was slightly unsettling to our Protestant sensibilities since most modern Protestant denominations have rejected the notion of praying to God through saints.

And yet, who were we to reject someone else's spirituality? We wanted to be open to learning new things, but it was too much at the moment.

"Would you mind if we left and went back upstairs to the lower basilica?" I asked. "This place makes me feel sad on so many levels."

"Gladly. Let's walk around behind the tomb so we don't miss anything and then go."

I was glad we did, because there we found the tombs of Brothers Rufino, Angelo, Masseo, and Leo, the first of the Franciscans. It seemed right that they were all buried here together. Knowing that somehow lifted my spirits a tiny bit.

We ascended the stairs to the lower basilica where we took time to look at the astounding frescos—some of the life of Jesus and others of the life of Francis. The colors were muted golds with vibrant blues and reds. We visited the chapel of St. Martin of Tours and of Mary Magdalene. Then we approached the altar area with its vaulted left and right transepts. It was the most beautiful presbytery I had ever seen.[18] The first fresco in the presbytery, called the "Allegory of Poverty," was my favorite, depicting Christ performing the wedding Mass of Francis and Lady Poverty.

But my favorite part of all were the relics in the chapterhouse room.[19] Placed in the room were several items, from a horn given to Francis by the Sultan of Egypt to a chalice and paten Francis had used. But there were two items I could not take my eyes off of—his tunic, intentionally shaped like the Tau cross[20] and patched more times than I could count, and a draft of the *Divine Praises* authored by Francis and given to Brother Leo. The poem was beautiful. His handwriting was beautiful. But it was the signature, a Tau symbol made by Francis's own hand, which thrilled me. Somehow, it made Francis come to life more so than anything else I had experienced in Assisi.

We went back outside and climbed the exterior stairs to the upper basilica where we entered an even more spectacular space. It was strikingly beautiful, filled with light flowing through stained glass windows, and even more frescos. There were twenty-eight frescos in all. By the time we reached the seventh scene, I was thinking about the similarities between Francis and Paul again. This scene, which took place in 1209, showed a humble Francis kneeling before Pope Innocent III, receiving a half-hearted blessing that may or may not have made the Franciscans an official order of the Catholic Church. However, the men are shown tonsured in the picture, the symbol of the preacher, indicating at a minimum they were given permission to preach.

The story goes that during Francis's visit to Rome, Pope Innocent III initially turned Francis down saying, "My dear children, your life appears to me too severe. I see indeed that your fervor is too great for any doubt of you to be possible, but I ought to consider those who shall come after you, lest your mode of life should be beyond their strength."[21] In other words, he did not think Francis's way of utter poverty was exactly the way to run an order. The pope had a point. Begging for all of one's food, going barefoot,

---

18. The presbytery of a church building is the area where the officiating clergy stand during Mass.

19. A chapterhouse room is a large room that is generally located on the eastern wing of a cloister next to the church, big enough for the whole community to meet privately. Doors and windows are limited to ensure privacy from eavesdropping.

20. Francis proclaimed to his friars that their tunics represented the Tau cross not only by its shape, but it wrapped each friar in his life-long commitment to become a walking crucifix, the incarnation of a compassionate God.

21. Sabatier, *The Road to Assisi*, 54.

living without proper shelter, refusing winter clothing, and not receiving theological training were hard on the health and spiritual life of those committed to serving others. It did not help that on visits to Rome, Francis and his men refused to eat the fancy food they were served and to stay in the fancy quarters they were offered, thus offending their hosts.

Francis went away, disappointed, but later returned to the pope to try to convince him the Franciscans were "sons of the King of Kings" and should be recognized by the church. Again, the pope was less than enthusiastic, but this time sent Francis away with instructions to continue with what they were doing and to come back when the Franciscans had multiplied further. Somewhere along the line, either intentionally or unintentionally, the order merged into the church. Confirming this in the chapterhouse room is a document called *The Bull of Solet Annuere*. In this 1223 document, Pope Honorius III confirmed the Franciscans were an official order of the church fourteen years after Francis's initial inquiry.

Both Francis and Paul built Christian communities before ever consulting with the church leaders. You can imagine this was not exactly welcomed by church leaders who had come up through the ranks. The first rule of life Francis submitted to Rome, although it has been lost, was known to be extremely simple. It was likely just Jesus's instructions to the apostles—to minister to the world without payment, without handling money, and without bringing along any possessions.[22] All Francis wanted from the Pope was to agree that the Franciscans and their rule were indeed a valid part of the church. Francis did not seek money, land, or any type of support—just acknowledgement.

Both Paul and Francis wanted to fix the church. They also wanted their communities to be successful in living the Christian life. And in both cases, the leaders of the church agreed with their theology, yet at the same time, rejected their praxis. The Jerusalem Council agreed with Paul that the Christian life was by grace, but at the same time, the council slipped in four essential rules. Rome agreed Francis was right to follow the teachings of Jesus to go about the work of God without regard for materialism, but the church leaders, who lived in luxury, weren't about to agree Jesus wanted that for his whole church.

For Francis in particular, from the day the Franciscans came under the authority of Rome, the order degenerated. It became more and more unfaithful to its rule of poverty. Eventually, Francis would lose control of

22. Matt 10:5–15.

his order altogether. Paul would continue to have conflicts with the church too. Still they both desired to be part of the organized church.

Even so, Paul and Francis were outsiders. These two renegades showed little respect for the hierarchy of the church. Paul wrote that the leaders in Jerusalem "contributed nothing to him." Paul showed up preaching grace and teaching a way of living in the Spirit that tossed out not just Jewish tradition and Jewish religious rules, but religious rules of any kind. Francis showed up preaching a rule of poverty and claiming God had given him the responsibility of fixing the church. He strongly criticized the wealth of the church, as well as its lack of compassion for the poor.

Perhaps they continued to pursue a relationship with the leaders of the church simply because the Kingdom of God should be united. Perhaps fixing the church meant becoming a part of it, so that they might have a voice in it. Whatever it was that drove them, trying to become part of the organized church created heartache for both of them. The church, for obvious reasons, wrong as these reasons were, really didn't want either of them around to upset the status quo.

In the end, their messages would be distorted. Many in the first century church would distort and rewrite Paul's message, teaching while salvation was by grace, the Christian life meant following a set of Christian rules. Likewise, the thirteenth century church would encase both Francis's message and his body in the glamor and riches of a great basilica. Neither man would have been happy with the outcome.

The twenty-first century church continues to do the same thing, remembering Paul as the maker of rules—subjugating women and condemning homosexuality—not as one who taught his communities to listen to and obey the Spirit for themselves. Francis is remembered as a lover of animals. We celebrate him by bringing our pets to church for a blessing. But he was far more than just that. He was one who preached against materialism and sent his listeners out to be servants caring for the sick and the poor.

"We have rewritten them both so they are more palatable to our way of life."

"By the way," my husband leaned over, "There were no pets and no mention of blessing them today in Assisi." Then bringing us back to Francis and Paul my husband asked, "Is being rejected by the church necessary to live the Christian life?"

"I sure hope not, but more times than I'd like to think about, the church has rejected those God sent to fix it," I said with a deep sigh.[23]

"Yeah, America has succeeded in making Francis nothing more than a garden gnome instead of wrestling with the materialism he taught against and the servitude he promoted."

"You know, there is some part of being a garden gnome that Francis would have liked."

"True."

Living the Christian life was becoming more complicated, not less.

23. "The prophet is a fool. This man with God's Spirit is crazy" (Hos 9:7). "I send you prophets, sages, and scribes, some of whom you will kill and crucify, and some you will flog" (Mat 23:34).

Spiritual Practice 2
Enlightenment

FRANCIS RECITED THE PRAYER below during the period of time when he began to seek Christ and when he started his order. It is believed this is what he was praying when the Byzantine crucifix spoke to him in San Damiano. Jesus answered Francis, telling him to fix the church. At first Francis interpreted it to mean the physical church. Later on, he came to believe he was called to fix the spiritual church.

THE SAN DAMIANO PRAYER[1]

Most High, Glorious God, Enlighten the darkness of my heart And give me true faith, certain hope, And perfect charity, sense and knowledge. Lord, That I may carry out Your holy and true commands. Amen.

STEP 1

Find a quiet place to pray.

STEP 2

Pray the San Damiano prayer. Pray it slowly, thinking over each word.

---

1. St. Francis. *Francis of Assisi: Early Documents, Vol. 1, The Saint*, 40.

STEP 3

Meditate on what the Holy Spirit is calling you to do with your life. During your meditation, return to the prayer as needed. Journal your thoughts.

PART 3

The Way Found

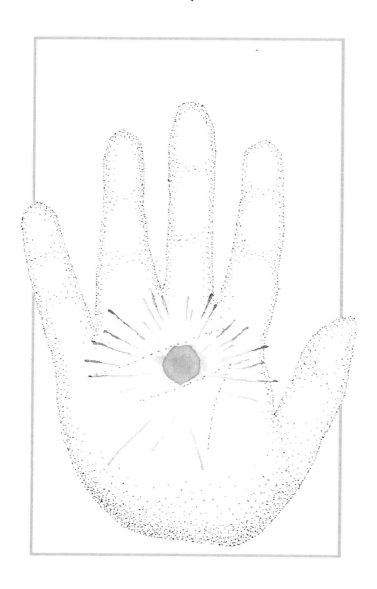

7

Acceptable to God

Galatians 2:15–16

Upon leaving the Basilica of St. Francis, we decided to walk the hour-long path down to the Basilica di Santa Maria degli Angeli in the valley. This was the blue-domed basilica we had watched light up the night before and the one Giovanni had pointed out to us earlier in the day. It literally encloses the first Franciscan headquarters, wrapping its glorious arms around the tiny Chapel of St. Mary, now referred to as the Porziuncola, and the Transito.

Our plan was to arrive in time to look around, stay for vespers, and then take a taxi back to our bed and breakfast. We retraced our steps on the Via Frate Elia through the lovely streets of Assisi, passing *ristoranti*, fine art galleries—my favorite of which was still the one with the flying monks—and *chincaglieria*, or trinket shops. Even the trinket shops looked inviting as we glanced inside the ancient stone buildings.

Before long the street turned into Piazza di Porta San Pietro where we passed under a city gate and found ourselves outside the walls of Assisi. A short jaunt down the Viale Guglielmo Marconi and we stumbled upon the stairs to a brick footpath we would follow the rest of the way. The sign said Via Padre Giovanni Principe.

My husband, once again with his perfect—yet annoying—Italian accent, read the sign and then translated it for me, "The street of Father Giovanni Prince."

"Father and Prince? What does that mean?" I asked.

"It is a sign Giovanni is going to show up here any moment!" my husband mused. Then, thinking I wouldn't notice, I caught him looking around for Giovanni.

"Hmmm." I said, letting him know I'd caught him looking.

"What? Where? He's here isn't he?" asked my husband—eyes darting down the slope ahead of us, searching for any sign of the little monk.

"I don't see him!" I giggled, "But honestly, he freaks me out a little too. It did just occur to me as you read the sign that Giovanni was Francis's given name."

"Oh that's right," he said with his eyes growing wider. "Are you thinking Giovanni is the ghost prince of St. Francis?"

My husband was kidding, of course, but at the same time, I knew him well enough to know he would be hoping it might be true. He and I both love a good mystery. One with a ghost would absolutely complete our little adventure in Italy.

"Hardly what I'm saying. But why don't you pinch Giovanni next time we see him to make sure?" I egged him on.

"I will."

"Okay then. But I gotta tell ya, this footpath isn't named after Prince Francis. It's named after Father Giovanni Principe. He was a twentieth century Franciscan monk who led the Istituto Serafico Per Sordomuti E Per Ciechi"

"The what? Woman, was that supposed to be Italian coming out of your mouth?"

"Maybe," I feigned being insulted. "You know you're only twenty-three percent Italian."

"Oh come on . . . how do you know anything about Father Giovanni Principe?"

"There's another sign behind you," and pointing eastward and down the hill I added, "And there is the *istituto*."

Turning, he read the sign, "Istituto Serafico Per Sordomuti E Per Ciechi," correcting my accent and pronunciation at the same time. "It's a school for blind and deaf students."

"A very Franciscan thing for Father John Prince to do! Just look at Francis's legacy! It's *meraviglioso!*"

"You pronounced that wrong too," he heckled me.

"No I didn't," I said confidently, knowing I probably did.

From there we followed the brick footpath down the steep hill to the beautiful flat valley where red poppies had bloomed in the spring, but were now spent from the summer sun. Turning around there were glorious views of Assisi behind us on the hill. The enormous basilica and surrounding buildings were even more spectacular from this vantage point. For the first time, we could see the fifty-three tall Romanesque arches, which supported the Sacro Convento attached to the basilica. It was truly an architectural achievement.

Hungry, we noticed a sign to an elegant but rustic farmhouse with the tagline written in English: "An Assisi Country House and Restaurant."

"Let's see if they'll feed us," suggested my husband.

Within minutes, we were sitting on a garden terrace with spectacular panoramic views of the ancient city, enjoying a delicious lunch of pasta and salad. The owner, an older Italian man with soft white hair, thick grey eyebrows, and brown eyes that twinkled, presided over every aspect of our meal, asking us all about our journey.

After listening attentively to our story, he was anxious to tell us the history of his country house. "You have heard of Francis's last days, no? Francis had been brought back to Assisi to die. He was kept against his will in the luxurious home of the bishop while the city awaited his death."

The owner paused, shaking his head as if he had personally experienced the pain of Francis's last days trapped with the bishop instead of his brothers. Then he went on, "But Francis, he sang at all hours of the day and night."

With that, the man began to sing, demonstrating just how loudly an Italian intent on exasperating those around him could belt out his oeuvre. "It's annoying, no?"

My hands had instinctively gone to my ears. My husband answered for us, "*Molto!*"

"The bishop begged Francis to stop, but Francis would not. Not only was he determined not to die without joy, it was his plan not to give the bishop any peace so he might be allowed to leave. The bishop, exhausted from lack of sleep, finally agreed to let Francis go home to the Porziuncola."

"That is where we are headed next!" I interjected.

"*Bene! Bene!*" he responded and then continued his story. "The brothers went into Assisi to fetch Francis in a cart. He was blind and so weakened by his illness he could not walk." The owner pointed to the ground at our feet. His eyes filled with tears as he finished his story. "When he was half-way to the Porziuncola . . . ." The owner stopped, overcome with emotion.

"This is halfway? Right here?" I asked, trying to interpret his emotional reaction and get him to finish the story.

"Si!" He nodded his head, then dramatically added, "*San Francesco* asked his brothers to turn him toward Assisi. Even though he couldn't see his beloved city, he raised his hands to bless it. He said his final goodbye right here on this ground." [1]

The owner held onto an empty chair at our table to steady himself, then with the other hand, crossed himself. After a moment, he wiped his face with a towel tucked into his belt, encouraged us to enjoy our lunch, and rushed back to the kitchen.

My husband leaned toward me so he could whisper, "Do you think he tells that story to every guest who eats here and do you think he cries every time?"

"I don't know, but I read about the incident he spoke of—Francis asking to be turned back toward the city to bless it one last time—that took place at the Hospital of the Carceri, which was likely attached to Santa Maria Maddalena, a tiny church also in the valley, a good thirty minute walk from here." [2]

"Is it half way to the Porziuncola too?"

"Yes, not the most direct way, but who knows what roads and paths actually existed in Francis's day. They were pulling a dying man in a cart. I guess they went the smoothest way, not the fastest."

"So you think the owner made that up?" laughed my husband.

Before I could answer, the owner was back. "I have a message for you," he said as he bowed.

"For us?" my husband expressed the confusion we both felt.

"You know Giovanni?"

"We do. Do you?" inquired my husband as he sat up straight and looked around for Giovanni.

"Everyone with a pure heart knows Giovanni!" the owner exclaimed. "He says to take your time and he will find you at the Santa Maria degli Angeli." Before we could respond, the owner was off to greet a family who had also arrived for lunch.

---

1. The words of Francis's last blessing are found at the beginning of chapter 5 of this book.

2. Sabatier, *The Road to Assisi*, 154.

"I have no words," my husband mused. Neither did I.

We finished lunch and as we were paying, the owner gave us a brown takeaway bag packed with food. Giovanni was written across the bag in black ink.

"Please give this to Giovanni," he requested.

We walked around the country house admiring the gardens. Colorful flowers and perfectly formed vegetables grew in meticulously groomed patches everywhere we looked. Then we walked the rest of the way on the now flat brick path to the Basilica of the Angels.

"Tell me more about Paul," asked my husband.

"Really? You never tire of hearing about the classes I'm planning?"

Taking my hand he said, "It's still a twenty minute walk and I married you because you're smart."

"And here I thought you loved me for my good looks?"

He wrinkled his face smugly and shook it to say no.

"My money?"

"There's money? Still no."

With that, I began telling him about my latest ponderings. "Paul wrote about a doctrine called *dikaioutai,* which is often translated justification. It is related to the question we have been asking about how to live the Christian life. To be justified by God means to be acceptable to God. Paul believed we are acceptable to God simply because Jesus was acceptable to God. Justification had nothing to do with being good enough or following a list of rules or even agreeing on the details of theology. The faithfulness of Jesus—Jesus's righteousness, his obedience even to the point of death on the cross—makes us righteous."

I stopped walking long enough to pull my smart phone from my backpack. I used an app to bring up Galatians, "Look, I've been struggling with these verses."

We ourselves are Jews by birth and not Gentile sinners; yet we know that a person is justified[3] not by the works of the law but through faith in Jesus Christ.[4] And we have come to believe in Christ Jesus, so that we might be justified by faith in Christ,[5] and not by doing

---

3. The word translated as justified was a legal term meaning all the charges against us have been forgiven.

4. "Through faith in Jesus Christ" could be translated "through the faithfulness of Jesus Christ."

5. Similar to the preceding comment, "By faith in Jesus Christ" could be translated

> the works of the law, because no one will be justified by the works of
> the law. (Gal 2:15–16)

"Paul's letter isn't just about waving them away from Jewish religious law. He is waving them away from *all* religious laws," I said.

"How do you know?'

"Two things. First, when describing the law, Paul does not use the word for the Torah. The Greek literally says 'works of law' making it general religious law, not 'works of *the* law' meaning *the* Jewish law, or Torah."

"So we're not justified by any set of religious rules, including the Torah?"

"Paul's gospel doesn't require we keep a list of rules. Christ has done everything necessary for our justification."

"So no rules. Do whatever you want—live however you want? And that's okay?" my husband questioned.

"Well, you can understand why the translators leaned toward the interpretation that Paul was rejecting just the Jewish law and not all religious rules. Paul's message was shocking. To say there is no set of rules we can follow to make ourselves acceptable to God takes away the power of the church leaders to control people."

"Do you realize this is a complete theological break with most of Christianity today?" my husband asked. "Also with most other world religions, which require the adherence to a set of religious rules in order to be acceptable to God?"[6]

"I do. It makes Christianity distinctly different."

"How are we to live the Christian life?" my husband repeated our quest.

"Not by following a list of rules! But that's just the first thing about this verse that has me doing some thinking. There's a second thing too."

"Rock my world, woman!"

"Well, faith is an important concept to Paul. But to Paul, faith isn't believing in something that can't be proven. Faith is our response to Christ's faithfulness. We are saved by faith not works, meaning we are saved by

---

"by the faithfulness of Jesus Christ."

6. McGee states that Christianity doesn't require we keep a list of rules since Christ has already done everything. McGee, *The Epistle to the Galatians*, 160. Peterson agrees with McGee writing that a better translation would be "a person is not justified by rule keeping." Peterson, *Traveling Light*, 71.

Christ's faithfulness.[7] All we can truly do on our own is to respond with a 'thank you.' This changes my understanding of Paul's writings. "

He tilted his head confused, "Show me the verses."

I pointed on my smartphone, "See this—here: 'Faith in Jesus Christ' could correctly be translated 'faith of Jesus Christ' meaning that we aren't justified by our faith in Jesus, but by Jesus's faithfulness.[8]

He tilted his head again still confused, "Read the whole verse using this possible translation."

"Okay. 'A person is justified not by the works of law, but by the faith of Jesus Christ' or in better English: 'A person is made acceptable to God not by keeping any set of religious rules, but by the faithfulness of Jesus Christ.'"

"So even our faith is not necessary, because Jesus was faithful in our place?" posited my husband.

"Listen to the verse after that one if you continue to use 'faithfulness of Jesus' instead of 'faith in Jesus.' 'And we have come to believe in Christ Jesus, so that we might be justified by the faithfulness of Jesus Christ.'"

"It is the faithfulness of Jesus that *might* justify us?" asked my husband.

"No, actually the translators added *might* too. Here's what I think Paul was saying . . ."

> A person is not made acceptable to God by following any religious law, but through the faithfulness of Jesus Christ. And we have come to believe in Christ Jesus who makes us acceptable to God by the faithfulness of Christ. (Gal 2:16)[9]

"That is shocking. Jesus has the faith for us?" questioned my husband.

"There is an argument to be made for that case. And if you think this is shocking to the two of us, then think how those rule followers, who were insisting the gentiles follow the Jewish law, felt hearing it. They had a completely different theological view on justification. They believed in Jesus, but they believed they were made holy by their own faith in Christ and by keeping the Torah—or at least some portion of it. It would blow their minds to think it was Jesus's faith alone that made them holy."

"So is Paul saying *everyone* is saved because of the faith of Jesus?"

---

7. Paul wrote, "For by grace you have been saved through faith, and this is not your own doing; it is the gift of God—not the result of works, so that no one may boast." Eph 2:8–9

8. Gal 2:15

9. Author's translation.

"I don't think Paul intended to be answering a question about salvation. First, he was writing to those who were followers of Christ already. Secondly, Jews didn't really have the concept of individual salvation. They weren't 'saved' because they personally believed a correct theology, led a righteous life, or did the right set of good deeds. Salvation was a community issue where priests made a yearly sacrifice that covered everyone's transgressions. Paul doesn't begin to address this."

"Okay, but then why would anyone go to the effort of leading a righteous life and doing a good set of deeds if not for salvation?"

"What did both Paul and Francis share? The *desire* to follow Jesus. The Holy Spirit lived in both of them and filled them with the *desire* to do the work of God."

"But why did these rule followers, bent on circumcising all of the male gentile Christians, want to continue following a tedious, long list of rules?"

"They wanted to keep their Jewish heritage. And they thought following the rules forced God to bless them in this world and in the next. They believed if they were good enough, God would have to bless them. That is not an uncommon belief among Christians today."

We walked a few steps in silence, when something occurred to me, "If you want to tie Galatians to salvation, read this." This time I pulled up a page from a commentary on my Kindle.

> Our salvation took place at the crucifixion when Jesus appropriated us and took us up into his death.[10] It is not a matter of our reception of Christ, but of Christ's appropriation of us: he grasps us and enfolds us within his own history, putting us to death so that we may be raised to life. And yet, we are set free for a faithful response to God's faithfulness and this is indeed our own proper faithfulness, our own decision and act.[11]

"The Christian life is a faithful response to Jesus's faithfulness," I summarized.

"What is a faithful response? Is that our answer to living the Christian life?"

"I would say a faithful response is being like Jesus, who allowed the Holy Spirit to give him the desire to obey God, the wisdom to know how, and the strength to do it."

---

10. Appropriated means to have taken something for a specific purpose without the owner being aware. We were with Jesus on the cross without even being aware.

11. Bird, *The Faith of Jesus Christ*, 301.

"How do we get the desire, the wisdom, and the strength to do that day in and out?"

"I think Paul is going to tell us, but I am not there yet."

"And Francis? What did he believe about justification?"

"I would guess he believed one must not only have faith in Jesus, but to be right before God, one must also follow 'the rules' he believed Christ gave to the disciples—the same rules Christ spoke to him directly at Mass that day in the Chiesa di Santa Maria degli Angeli. Remember Jesus appeared to him as the priest was reading Jesus's instructions to the apostles in Matthew.[12] So like the leader of any holy order, Francis wrote down what he believed were the rules Jesus expected his order to follow. Over the years, the Franciscan Rule of Life expanded beyond Matthew."

"Paul wouldn't have liked any rule of life."

"Nope. I think he would've said Francis was wrong to think Jesus was making a new set of Christian rules that must be followed. Paul probably would have said Jesus was giving guidelines to those particular disciples for that particular occasion, not a law for all the followers of Jesus."

"But Francis was this incredible man. Look at the positive impact he had—has—on the world." My husband was turned around looking up the hill and pointing, not to the Basilica of St. Francis, but to the institute for deaf and blind children. "How could a man have gotten it all wrong whose sons are still—eight hundred years later—taking care of those in need?"

"He didn't get it ALL wrong. God works through human imperfection all the time. Paul wasn't any more perfect than Francis. But they would've differed. One important thing is that both Paul and Francis believed they had received revelations from Jesus himself."

"Did they?"

"I really do think so. But don't ask me to explain why they settled on fundamentally different theological interpretations."

Finally, we arrived at the basilica. Lo and behold, ahead of us in the courtyard, sitting on a bench, was Giovanni. We both laughed when his short little body stood up and began its larger than life wave toward us. The man was nothing if not happy.

We delivered his bag of food and exchanged pleasantries as if we were longtime friends. Then my husband motioned for us to sit down and restarted our conversation, framing it as a question for Giovanni, "So Francis believed one must give up all material belongings and keep a rule of

12. Matt 10:5–15.

poverty while serving others in order to fully live the Christian life. Paul, on the other hand, believed keeping any set of religious rules was to reject the grace Christ offered us. He believed the Christian life must be lived by faith in Christ. Who was right?"

Giovanni hopped to his feet and turned to face us. With great gusto, he said, "Let me tell you a story!" It was again a treat to be entertained as this unusual little man began his story.

After Francis lost his authority over the Franciscan order, he continued to live at the Porziuncola with the brothers, but obviously, he was no longer in charge. It was no surprise or shock that Francis was not himself—he was feeling deeply grieved. He was also confused as to why God would have allowed this to happen. The church authorities had crushed all of his hopes and dreams. Nevertheless, he stayed, hoping to set an example of obedience—more to the rule of poverty than to the new leadership.

Watching the order move away from his strict rule of poverty to a still simple, but more practical, way of living was almost more than Francis could bear. Most of the brothers continued to look to Francis for leadership and wanted to please him. So one day a novice, who had gotten permission to own a psalter[13] from the minister general, the priest assigned to the order, went to Francis to make sure it would be okay with him too. He approached Francis for his permission three times. The first time, Francis said no. He insisted that resisting owning material goods was a battle the novice must fight for Christ.

The second time, Francis said no again. This time Francis pointed out that once the novice owned a psalter, he would then want to own other books and one thing would lead to another. Perhaps then, the novice would think he was so important he would demand the other brothers carry his breviary for him.[14]

Giovanni was extremely animated during the story, walking back and forth as if acting it out on a stage. For the finale, Giovanni sat in front of a pretend fire warming his hands while narrating, "The discussion with the novice upset Francis so much he stood up from the fire, grabbed ashes from it, and scattered them over the novice's head."

As Giovanni said this, he stood to dump a pretend handful of ashes on my husband's head and then ruffled his hair. It was such an encroachment into my husband's personal space I could not control my laughter.

13. A psalter is a book containing just the Psalms.
14. A breviary is a book that contains liturgical texts.

My husband looked over at me with his eyebrows raised and began to straighten his hair.

But my laughter did not phase Giovanni. He paused only long enough to get our full attention again. "The third time the novice showed up, Francis gave in." Giovanni lowered his head, expressing how terrible Francis felt. "Francis was giving into everything he had struggled against. He told the novice to follow whatever the minister general told him to do."

Giovanni sat back down on the sidewalk in front of us with his hand over his heart. "The novice left, but in just moments Francis realized what he had done and followed him crying."

Then Giovanni raised his voice pretending to be Francis, "It is not right that you would own anything, but your clothing."[15]

My husband, still not completely composed from having his hair ruffled, returned to his original question, "So Paul had his theology of Christian living and Francis had his. Both contributed much to the world. So how am I to live the Christian life?"

"I cannot tell you *what* is right for you. But I can tell you *how* you can know what is right for you," answered Giovanni as he led us into the basilica.

"Tell us," I begged. But before he could answer, the spectacular Basilica di Santa Maria degli Angeli opened before us. Down the center aisle, some distance away, was the little fourth century chapel, which legend claims once held relics from the grave of the Blessed Virgin Mary and from which came the sound of angels singing. The chapel's front exterior was now decorated with frescos. My husband and I fell silent as we walked the center aisle toward it. By the time we overcame our amazement, Giovanni had disappeared into thin air.

In silence, we prayed inside the tiny chapel. Then we visited the Transito where Francis had asked to be stripped naked and laid on the ground to die in order to leave this world in complete poverty. There I meditated on Francis's unyielding desire to be counted as righteous before God. I prayed I would have that desire too. The hours flew by as we soaked up the atmosphere and the lessons available to us throughout the basilica.

By the time we reached the *roseto*, or rose garden, afternoon was turning to evening though the sun would not set for some time. This was the garden where Francis had thrown himself naked into the rose bushes, wishing to do penitence for having doubts and temptations. It was there we

15. Sabatier, *The Road to Assisi*, 113.

realized that we had not spoken to each other since entering the basilica. I think neither of us had wanted to break the numinous feeling surrounding us.

"Notice the rose bushes have no thorns," I said to my husband. "Apparently, they fell off when Francis tried to hurt himself by throwing himself into them."

"Was he being faithful to the faithfulness of Christ when he tried to hurt himself?" asked my husband.

"I think he thought he was at the time. But on his deathbed, he confessed to having sinned grievously against his body."[16]

"It's hard to believe this man—with the strongest of desires to serve Jesus—didn't have the perfect understanding of the Christian life," my husband remarked.

"We don't have to get it all right in order to live the Christian life. Jesus got it right for us."

"It is more about having the desire to walk with Jesus, isn't it?"

"And yet, we can't manufacture that desire."

The bells for vespers began to ring and we went back inside. A line of Franciscan monks proceeded in after we were seated. With the sun starting to set, vespers began.

16. Brother Leo, *Legend of the Three Companions*, Kindle Location 198.

8

Crucified with Christ

Galatians 2:17–21

I WAS SITTING ON our rooftop terrace in the dark. I had woken up happy in the early hours of the morning. Although I tried to fall back to sleep, I finally decided to get out of bed. My thoughts led me back to Paul.

But if, in our effort to be justified in Christ, we ourselves have been found to be sinners, is Christ then a servant of sin? Certainly not! But if I build up again the very things that I once tore down, then I demonstrate that I am a transgressor. For through the law I died to the law, so that I might live to God. I have been crucified with Christ.[1] (Gal 2:17-19)

In these verses I found the only hint I could find as to why the Galatians might have been vulnerable to turning away from the gospel Paul had taught them: "If in our effort to be justified (made acceptable to God) in Christ, we ourselves have been found to be sinners." I wondered if there had been some bad behavior among the Galatians—behavior the community wasn't prepared to deal with. In other words, they had been going along living the Christian life and obeying the Spirit, but then there was a failure of some sort. Someone sinned in a way that deeply hurt the community. So when

---

1. The Greek word translated "crucified with" literally means "co-crucified" or "crucified together."

the rule followers showed up, the Galatians were primed to be convinced this failure would not have happened if they had had a set of rules to follow.

The problem with that kind of thinking is fourfold. First, anyone can keep a list of religious rules. They do not need to have a relationship with Jesus. Keeping a set of rules is how most world religions claim one pleases God. But Jesus taught the entire law could be summed up by loving God and neighbor.

> "Teacher, which commandment in the law is the greatest?" Jesus said to him, "'You shall love the Lord your God with all your heart, and with all your soul, and with all your mind.' This is the greatest and first commandment. And a second is like it: 'You shall love your neighbor as yourself.' On these two commandments hang all the law and the prophets." (Mat 22:36–40)

In other words, people do the will of God because their heart desires to love God and others, not because there is a specific rule that threatens them. If someone is sinning, it is his or her heart that needs an adjustment. Making a rule against sin neither stops nor forgives sin.

Second, loving God and others is complicated. There are nuances and exceptions to almost every rule. No list of rules can address them all. Nor can the rules direct us on how to go about loving God and others. However, the living Spirit of God can. The law is not a good substitute for being guided directly by God.

Third, when people have a rule, they tend to do only enough to say they have kept the rule. Jesus addresses this in the Sermon on the Mount.[2] He lists a number of things the Torah commanded like don't murder, don't commit adultery, don't swear falsely, etc. Then Jesus shocks everyone by telling the crowd these rules do not go far enough. Not only should they not murder, they shouldn't even use words that condemn. Not committing adultery isn't enough either, because they shouldn't even lust. Forget not swearing falsely, they shouldn't swear at all. The Christian life goes further than the law could imagine simply because the law can't imagine.

Fourth, when God's acceptance hinges on following a list of rules, it becomes of the utmost importance that one has the right list of rules. Instead of pursuing the Holy Spirit's guidance, much time must be spent getting the rules right. It becomes such an all-encompassing pursuit that living in the Spirit is completely forgotten.

2. Matt 5:22–48.

Whatever has happened in the Galatian community, it has shaken their confidence in Paul's teachings. To address this, Paul lays out a question before them. The following modern interpretation of these verses spoke to me:

> Have some of you noticed that we are not perfect? And are you ready to make the accusation that since people like me, who seek to be justified by Christ, aren't perfectly virtuous, Christ must therefore be an accessory to sin? The accusation is frivolous. If I was "trying to be good," I would be reconstructing the same old barn that I tore down and acting as a charlatan. What actually took place is this: I tried keeping rules and working my head off to please God, and it didn't work; so I quit so that I could simply be, so I could live in harmony with God.[3]

I would go a step further than the author of that interpretation has gone. I would add that it is our obedience to the Holy Spirit's leading that puts us in harmony with God and where we find peace even in the midst of a storm. But the author is right: the Christian life is a life of peace, not a life of striving to be good enough.

In these verses, Paul confirmed neither he nor the Galatians would live the Christian life perfectly. They would not follow the Spirit without failing. And yet, they were still acceptable in God's eyes. Not because of what they did, but because of what Christ did. This in no way meant Christ's work had given a thumbs up to living in a way that hurt God and others. Instead, the Holy Spirit strengthened the followers of Jesus by giving them the desire, the wisdom, and the strength to love God and others—including forgiving the failures of ourselves and others.

Paul had tried to be good enough by keeping the Jewish religious law perfectly. He was a failure. Instead of loving God and others, he took part in the murder of Jewish Christians. He would not go back to that way of living. It did not please God.

Just then, my husband woke. Realizing I wasn't next to him, he called to me.

"I'm outside. I think I had a dream."

"A nightmare?" He stood, a shadow, at the door.

"No, I felt happy. But I don't really remember. It had something to do with the night we spent at the guest house in La Verna."

---

3. Peterson, *Traveling Light*, 72.

"Near the end of our first week on the Cammino di Assisi?" he asked as he sat down next to me.

I unwrapped the blanket around me and covered us both. The gold lights of Assisi flickered both on the hill above us and in the valley below us. It was still dark, but the moon illuminated the clouds that sat just below the Basilica of St. Clare, blanketing some of the valley below.

"Yes. Where Francis received the stigmata," I answered. "That place felt so holy as we walked down the outdoor corridor to the Santuario della Verna."

"I know what you mean, but my gosh! I wish the Italians would not cover every sacred thing with a dang church building. Francis had gone to this remote place—a rugged, rocky outcrop—to be with God. But what do these Italians do? They build a church over it. It no longer resembles the primitive, rustic feeling of God's creation that Francis saw and felt that day."

"Think this through with me," I said. "Francis, who was sick and already knew he was dying, had gone to the top of what was then known as Monte Alverna to spend time on the magnificent land that had been given to the Franciscans. On the top of the massive sheer rock outcrop, the brothers had formed a primitive hermitage out of equally primitive huts. When Francis arrived, he separated himself from the brothers and went to the edge of the rock to be alone with God and pray."

"You know, I think we best experienced what it was like for Francis when we exited the chapel—the one toward the guest house where we could lean over the railings and see the long distant views."

"True. You're really stuck on the backdrop right now, aren't you?" I teased. "Are you listening to me?"

"I'm not awake yet. But the feeling of thinness between this world and the next was strong there."

"It felt like we were standing on the edge of eternity." I paused remembering the feel and smell of the fresh air, "Anyway, listen to me. Remember during the night, Francis had a vision of a winged seraph enfolding a crucified man who had the face of Jesus."[4]

"Yes, I remember the story. A crucified man and a winged seraph would give anyone a nightmare but you," he teased, still not tracking with me.

---

4. Brother Leo, *Legend of the Three Companions*, Kindle location 742.

"Okay. Pay attention. Francis often had visions. But afterwards this time, Francis had Christ's wounds on his own hands, feet, and side. He had received the stigmata."

"Yep. I'm with you chief." He teased me, calling me chief whenever he thought I was being bossy.

I passed my Kindle to my husband pointing at a particular passage, "Now read that verse from Galatians."

"'I have been crucified with Christ.' Are you saying Paul received the stigmata too?"

I took back my Kindle and scrolled down a couple of chapters to Gal 6:17 and then handed it back to my husband who read, "From now on, let no one make trouble for me; for I carry the marks of Jesus branded on my body."

The word translated 'marks' is the Greek word *stigmata*. It is the only time the word *stigmata* appears in scripture. Scholars—mostly Catholics—believed Paul had received what we define as the stigmata today—the actual wounds of Christ. But Protestant scholars generally believe the original meaning of the word had to do with the branding of slaves, not the mystical marking of exceptionally holy people.[5] Protestants usually accept Paul was talking about the scars from the beatings he had suffered many times for preaching the gospel."

Taking my Kindle again and finding Paul's second letter to the Corinthians, I read from another letter of Paul's where he seemed to be talking about the marks of Jesus in a spiritual rather than physical way:

> We are afflicted in every way, but not crushed; perplexed, but not driven to despair; persecuted, but not forsaken; struck down, but not destroyed; always carrying in the body the death of Jesus, so that the life of Jesus may also be made visible in our bodies. For while we live, we are always being given up to death for Jesus's sake, so that the life of Jesus may be made visible in our mortal flesh. (2 Cor 4:8–11)

My husband commented, "Paul understood that suffering as we live the Christian life is inevitable, but he wasn't suggesting we should desire

---

5. Aquinas explained that the original meaning of the word stigmata was "strictly speaking, certain marks branded on one with a hot iron; as when a slave is marked on the face by his master, so that no one else will claim him, but quietly let him remain with the master whose marks he bears." Aquinas, *Commentary on the Letters of Saint Paul to the Galatians*, Un-paginated commentary on Gal 6:16–18.

suffering just for the sake of suffering, right? He doesn't mean that suffering makes us more holy or that it's a sign we're more holy."

"I would agree. I see no evidence in scripture that Christians should pursue suffering. And I don't think our answer to how we live the Christian life is to go around trying to find ways to suffer."

"That's good. But Francis. Oh boy—what a harsh way to follow Christ."

"Seriously. What a pain!" I tried to be funny with no success. "Thomas of Celano wrote that when Francis received the stigmata, Francis saw himself humbly 'decorated beyond the glory and honor of all others.'[6] Yet, he tried to keep his wounds, which never healed, a secret as much as possible."

"Did the wounds hurt?"

"Apparently so. Once Rufino touched the scar on Francis's side by accident and it was very painful to Francis. But that was part of the deal. Francis wanted to suffer for Christ—he believed he needed to and it was his privilege."

"What do you think about the stigmata?"

"I don't really know and I am not sure it matters. The church verified the marks on Francis's body at his death, but it is very likely Paul was just speaking figuratively about his own body."

Either way, Paul believed the life of a Christian was completely enfolded into the death and life of Christ. Similar to someone saying they are the hands and feet of Christ. Or as Jesus put it, "I am the vine, you are the branches. Those who abide in me and I in them bear much fruit, because apart from me you can do nothing" (John 15:5). Jesus's followers were (and are) enabled to do the work of God as the lifeblood of the vine, the Holy Spirit, pumps through them. This also complements what Paul wrote:

> It is no longer I who live, but it is Christ who lives in me. And the life I now live in the flesh I live by faith in the Son of God, who loved me and gave himself for me.[7] I do not nullify the grace of God; for if justification comes through the law, then Christ died for nothing. (Gal 2:20–21)

"Here's a weird question."

"Just one?" I teased.

"So if Christ lives in us, are we still ourselves?"

6. Celano, *The Francis Trilogy*, 103–105.

7. Betz writes that the divine life, which the Christian receives through the indwelling of Christ, expresses itself as faith. Betz, *Galatians*, 125.

"Yes. When we are living the Christian life, it is Christ's work in us, but it is also truly our work. We are co-creators with God as the Spirit fashions us from the faithful existence of Christ."[8]

"The faithful existence of Christ? Did you coin that?"

"Hardly, but I can't remember who did at this wee hour of the morning. I'd like to go back to sleep."

"Me too." He stood unwrapping his side of the blanket and handed it to me. As we climbed into our cozy bed, he said, "Perhaps the key to the Christian life is continuing the life of Christ—being his hands and feet."

I drifted into peaceful sleep, but when I woke, my husband had showered, dressed, and was sitting on the terrace with chocolate croissants on a tray. "Any more dreams?" he asked.

"Not that I remember," I stretched as I tried to shake the cobwebs from my mind. "Hey! Today is the annual *Fiera di San Francesco*![9] Vendors from all over Italy will be here winding their way through the medieval alleyways selling their crafts."

"Fun! Shopping!" he said sarcastically.

"Don't make fun of me. If you are nice, I might buy you a tau cross."

"Okay then! Let's visit the vendors as we walk to the Rocca Maggiore castle at the top of the hill. I just checked and it's open today."

"Perfect."

The market and castle felt like a fun distraction from my studies. The market was colorful with everything from embroidered linen scarves to tau crosses carved from Assisi olive trees that hung on leather strings to be worn around one's neck. I did in fact buy one for my husband, which he wears even to this day. In addition, there were Italian cheeses, honeys, olives, beautiful dresses and shirts, with no end of St. Francis trinkets, including St. Francis bobblehead dolls.

We took our time, sampling everything as we went. In the afternoon, we reached Rocca Maggiore. The main attraction that day was the city market so, with the exception of the young woman selling tickets at the entrance to the castle, we were pretty much alone, making it exceptionally fun to explore. The castle had been built in the sixth century, so it was already old when Francis was born. Beneath the castle on its south hill were yellow flowers—weeds really—in glorious bloom. The castle had everything—a

---

8. Bird, *The Faith of Jesus Christ*, 307.

9. The *Fiera di San Francesco* is a lively open-air market that overruns the streets of Assisi once a year on the day after St. Francis's Feast Day celebrations.

round squat turret at the entrance, a tall castle keep at its center, a coat of arms carved into the stone wall with half human, half dragon beasts, several delightful courtyards, and then an extremely long above ground tunnel hidden in the city wall, complete with staggered bow loops for fighting.

We passed through the long tunnel to the outer rampart where we climbed up a tower. There we were rewarded with a phenomenal view of the Basilica of St. Francis to the southwest. To the north we could see all the way to Satriano. To the southeast was the magnificent Assisi in all of her glory. Without a doubt, it was the most beautiful city we had ever been in. At that height, unprotected from the elements, we were delighted by a chilly wind rushing around us, blaring its blustery song.

"What a great pilgrimage this has been!" shouted my husband as he wrapped his arms around me to protect me from being blown over the guardrail. "The best part was spending time together!"

"But we don't have a complete answer yet. Bits and pieces. The specifics aren't solidified in my mind yet." I sighed.

"Maybe Francis was right, we should seek to be martyrs. Let's see, how do we make someone so mad they kill us?"

"No thanks!"

Where my husband was going with Francis was curious. At first, Francis believed he must give up all material processions to be right with God, but somewhere along the line, he decided becoming a martyr would also please God and complete his service to God. It became so much of an obsession that at one point he up and left his order to go off to the Holy Land where he would try to convert the Sultan of Babylonia. He hoped the sultan would martyr him, but the sultan decided he liked Francis and they became friends. In fact, the sultan asked Francis to show him what he must do for salvation. Francis answered, "Do not let anything hinder your desires for faith, and when grace comes, God will find you with faith."[10] Francis believed in grace when it came to salvation. He just didn't think it was how you lived out the Christian life.

"So martyrdom is a nonstarter?" asked my husband.

"Yeah, I think you can cross that off your list!"

10. Celano, *The Francis Trilogy*, 324–325.

9

Paul Defends the Gospel
Galatians 3:1—4:31

ON THE WAY DOWN the hill from Rocca Maggiore, we took our time taking in the sunlit crooks and turns of the narrow Assisi streets while looking for a place to eat lunch. As we did, we passed the Cattedrale di San Rufino.[1] This was the young Francis's home church, as it were. While this church building may have been new in the twelfth century, a Christian community had existed here in Assisi as early as the third century. In fact, an even older church building had been on this spot for hundreds of years before Francis's birth.

There were several thought-provoking things about Francis's family church. It was named after St. Rufino, who had brought Christianity to Assisi, but not without problems. In 238, the Romans drowned him by tying a stone to his neck and throwing him in the Chiascio River that flows in the valley to the west of Assisi. His remains were buried in a Roman sarcophagus under the main altar. In addition, two lions, each in the process of eating a Christian—head first, no less—stand guard at the main entrance of the Cathedral.[2] The martyrdom theme must have captivated the young Francis. I wondered aloud what effect this had on Francis's desire to become a martyr himself.

---

1. See picture 32 in the appendix.
2. See picture 33 in the appendix.

"Kind of gruesome," remarked my husband. "Bet the young Francis loved it." My husband glanced above the lions to the rose window decorating the Romanesque architecture and took notice of a carved stone relief of Jesus enthroned between the sun and moon.[3] "Could this have been his inspiration for *Cantico del fratello sole e sorella luna*?"[4]

"The Canticle of Brother Sun and Sister Moon. Maybe so."

As we passed the church, I mentioned to my husband that after we got some lunch, I would like to come back here to work for a while. I liked sitting in the quietness of a church and studying. He was fine with that, saying he thought he would walk towards the basilica and look in the shops. He would come find me afterwards.

We had an excellent lunch in a *ristorante biologico* that served organic sandwiches of smoked cheese, red chicory, walnuts, and honey on fresh flat bread all sourced from a small nearby farm. Then I made my way back to San Rufino. The interior was cheerfully bright and I was greeted inside at the left of the entrance by a life size statue of Francis himself with both hands across his chest and a bowed head.[5] To the right of the entrance was the baptismal font where Francis's mother had brought him shortly after his birth to be baptized with the name Giovanni Bernadone, a name that would, in short order, be changed to Francesco by his father when he arrived home from his business travels.[6]

This was also the church where Francis, invited to preach, spoke so convincingly that a sixteen-year-old girl, Chiara Offreduccio, later to be known as *Santa Chiara* or St. Clare, would leave her noble family and follow him into a life of poverty and service.

Before I opened my laptop, I walked around absorbing the white walls and rectangles of glass floor that allowed one to peak underneath the church to see the remains of a Roman structure. The church was almost completely empty.

I had come to the portion of Galatians where Paul spent a great deal of time defending his theology. He began this section of his letter with an expression of frustration:

3. See picture 34 in the appendix.

4. Part of the translated lyrics can be found in Spiritual Practice 4 of this book.

5. See picture 35 in the appendix.

6. Francesco was an unusual choice for an Italian baby since it literally means Frenchman.

> You foolish[7] Galatians! Who has bewitched[8] you? It was before
> your eyes that Jesus Christ was publicly exhibited as crucified![9]—
> Gal 3:1

After Paul released this tension, he gave seven different arguments from seven different angles. As I read them, I came to find out that key to understanding Paul's arguments and theology was his use of the word promise. It is commonly thought that Paul was talking about the promise of salvation, but it was more than that.

Paul defined this promise in Galatians 3:14 when he wrote, "In Christ Jesus the blessing of Abraham might come to the Gentiles, so that we might receive the promise of the Spirit through faith." God had made a promise to Abraham, the ancient patriarch from whom all Jews trace their lineage. The promise included several things: God would be his god. God would give him land, heirs, and *the* heir (the Messiah). It would be through the Messiah that gentiles would be included in the promise. But the end result of the promise, as ancient prophets such as Ezekiel and Jeremiah would explain, was the sending of the Holy Spirit.[10] They told of a time when God would no longer be separated from us, but God's spirit would dwell within us. No longer would the Spirit be a temporary visitor in the lives of humanity, showing up for particularly important missions, but the Holy Spirit would now live permanently within the hearts of all believers. Of course, the promise of the Holy Spirit was fulfilled at Pentecost.

Most first century Jews would have disagreed with Paul's definition of the promise. Instead they believed the promise was more about the land and heirs—Jewish nationalism—than about the Spirit. In their minds, the function of the Messiah was to revitalize the Jewish nation, which at that time was overrun with Roman occupiers. However, because of Pentecost, the rule following Jewish nationalists could not deny the Holy Spirit was at least the result of the promise, if not the promise itself. So the Holy Spirit is where Paul focused his arguments.

---

7. The Greek word for foolish means thoughtless or unthinking.

8. Mesmerized might be a better word than bewitched. In other words, Paul is saying they are like a rabbit hypnotized by a snake. He would like them to take their eyes off the snake and focus on the gospel.

9. Jesus's body was not actually put on display in Galatia. A literal translation is "Jesus Christ was visually portrayed."

10. Ezk. 36:22–32 and Jer. 31:31–34.

I opened my laptop and started organizing my notes on the evidence Paul presented to the Galatians. But before I got very far, I heard someone sit down in the row of chairs which started directly behind my pew. In an empty cathedral that felt a little creepy—why sit so close to the only other person in the sanctuary? I tried to nonchalantly look behind me, pretending to look at the door, but I couldn't turn my head far enough to get a glimpse of whoever it was. I started back to work. Then the hair on my neck literally stood up as I heard words whispered slowly at the back of my head.

"Hello . . . I need the keys . . . to our room."

I put my laptop down, and turning around, glared at my husband. "You think you're so funny! You scared me to death! I might've screamed!"

"Did you think I was Giovanni?" he said, thrilled at having rattled me.

I squinted my eyes and scrunched my mouth in playful disgust, which quickly turned into a question of my own, "While you are here, there is something that will rattle your brain in Galatians. Got time to hear it?"

"I *am* on vacation for a few more days so I have all the time in the world."

"Ok—look at the verse at 3:1, 'It was before your eyes Jesus Christ was publicly exhibited as crucified!'"

"I didn't know Jesus's body was put on exhibit before he was buried. That's disturbing."

"It wasn't. Especially not in Galatia. Jesus died and was buried on the same day. Galatia was nine hundred miles from Jerusalem."

"So how did the Galatians see Jesus crucified?"

"Well, if I translate the verse this way, tell me what you think, 'before whose eyes Jesus Christ was *proegraphea* crucified."

"Photographed?"

"Yeah. The word means visually portrayed. One translation says 'a picture of his death.'"

"So where did they get a camera?"

"You tell me." I sat smiling at him while his brain turned it over.

"The Shroud of Turin?"[11]

"It's what all the Shroud of Turin conspiracy theorists have blogged about at one time or another."

11. The Shroud of Turin is a linen cloth kept in the Cathedral of St. John the Baptist in Torino, Italy. It bears the blood and negative image of a crucified man. Many believe this is the cloth that Jesus was wrapped in at his burial (John 20:6–9) and that the mysterious image was created as some kind of radiation was emitted from his body as he was resurrected from the dead.

"Seriously? There are Shroud of Turin conspiracy theorist bloggers?"

"Yep. Honestly, maybe I should call them enthusiasts."

"So is this evidence of the Shroud of Turin?"

"Your guess is as good as mine!"

With that he stood, popped both hands open beside his head as if to say his mind was blown, and left the church without saying goodbye.

In about five minutes, the cathedral doors opened again. I had pulled the keys to our bed and breakfast out of my backpack and without looking back toward him held them up smiling ear-to-ear as I kept working.

He snatched them from my hand and, knowing I had hoodwinked him, said, "Okay. You got me back for scaring you." Then I started working. When I get busy, I can work for hours. This was one of those times.

Here is the evidence Paul laid out before the Galatians—minus the possibility of the shroud, just because I wanted to be taken seriously by my students, who would no doubt find the shroud business over the top. I, however, loved the possibility the Shroud was legit. At any rate, Paul was focused on providing proof that following any set of religious rules was contrary to the Christian life.

PROOF 1: YOU RECEIVED THE SPIRIT BEFORE YOU HAD ANY INTENTION OF KEEPING A LIST OF RELIGIOUS RULES.

The only thing I want to learn from you is this: Did you receive the Spirit by doing the works of the law or by believing what you heard? Are you so foolish? Having started with the Spirit, are you now ending with the flesh? Did you experience so much for nothing?—if it really was for nothing. Well then, does God supply you with the Spirit and work miracles among you by your doing the works of the law, or by your believing what you heard? (Gal 3:2–5)

Paul contrasted Spirit with flesh. In this context, flesh meant anything we try to do ourselves in order to be acceptable to God—including trying to follow a set of religious rules. He pointed out that the Spirit came upon the Galatians before they ever even thought about following the Torah. This was important because the indwelling Spirit was (and is today) the mark of the follower of Jesus. In a letter to the Ephesians, Paul wrote, "When you had heard the word of truth, the gospel of your salvation, and had believed in him, you were marked with the seal of the promised Holy Spirit" (Eph 1:13).

Paul reminds the Galatians that they had received the Spirit—the living wisdom of God—and they had experienced the miracles of the Spirit—the living power of God. The Spirit had been a gift from God, not something they had to earn by keeping the law. Therefore, there was no reason for them to have thought that they must now start following a set of religious rules in order to live the Christian life and be acceptable to God.

Paul said something else that I found extraordinarily interesting, but which the translators glossed over. The translation has Paul asking, "Did you receive the Spirit by believing what you heard?" Yet, that isn't exactly what Paul said. Paul asked, "Did you receive the Spirit by hearing faith?" I think this is significant. We can't turn off our hearing. We hear because God speaks to us. We have faith because God gives it to us and we receive the Holy Spirit the same way. We literally can do nothing to earn or deserve God's gifts of faith or the Spirit. Receiving the Spirit spontaneously happens when we hear faith.

God loved the Galatians though they did not merit it. God forgave the Galatians for past, present, and future sins though they did not merit it. However, they had come to think they must follow a list of rules or else the Holy Spirit would no longer guide them or do miracles among them. That was bad theology.

PROOF 2: GOD'S PROMISE TO GIVE THE SPIRIT WAS A PROMISE FOR EVERYONE.

Just as Abraham "believed God, and it was reckoned to him as righteousness,"[12] so, you see, those who believe are the descendants of Abraham. And the scripture, foreseeing that God would justify the Gentiles by faith, declared the gospel beforehand to Abraham, saying, "All the Gentiles shall be blessed in you."[13] For this reason, those who believe are blessed with Abraham who believed.

For all who rely on the works of the law are under a curse[14]; for it is written, "Cursed is everyone who does not observe and obey all

12. Gen 15:6.

13. Gen 22:18.

14. Peterson interprets those who "rely on the works of the law" to be "anyone who

> the things written in the book of the law." [15,16] Now it is evident that no one is justified before God by the law; for "The one who is righteous will live by faith." [17] But the law does not rest on faith; on the contrary, "Whoever does the works of the law will live by them." [18] Christ redeemed [19,20] us from the curse of the law by becoming a curse for us—for it is written, "Cursed is everyone who hangs on a tree" [21]—in order that in Christ Jesus the blessing of Abraham might come to the Gentiles, so that we might receive the promise of the Spirit through faith. (Gal 3:6–14)

Abraham did not struggle to be right with God. He did not have to earn his relationship with God. He did not initiate his relationship with God. He did not have to be taught how to have faith or force himself to have faith. God gave him faith and God counted it as righteousness.

Paul quotes the Old Testament, "All the Gentiles shall be blessed in you." [22] To the first century Jew, the phrase meant God tangentially blessed gentiles through the Jews. In other words, God created and maintained the world, because he loved the Jews, but sometimes their cultural achievements and scientific knowledge also benefited the gentiles despite their unworthiness.

However, Paul was standing this commonly held Jewish theology on its ear. Paul said scripture foresaw God would bless the gentiles through Jesus, who was Jewish. Gentiles were not second-class citizens in the Kingdom of God. The Messiah, who was Jesus, would redeem all people so all people could receive the Holy Spirit.

---

tries to live independently of God by his own effort." Peterson, *Traveling Light*, 85.

15. In this case, Paul is specifically referring to the Torah by using the Greek words translated "book of the law."

16. Deut 27:26.

17. Hab 2:4.

18. Lev 15:8.

19. Redeemed means to buy back—as in to buy back the freedom of one who has become enslaved. This is what Christ did for us on the cross.

20. Peterson teaches that in the pagan world, redemption was the process of freeing slaves. A free person would deposit the amount of money that the pagan priests required to free the slave. The pagan priests would say, "The God Apollo has purchased this slave and he is now free." Paul compared this to what Christ did for us. Peterson, *Traveling Light*, 116.

21. Deut 21:23.

22. Gen 22:18.

In addition, Paul said if they tried to live the Christian life by following the Torah, then they were living under a curse. This was partly because they must keep all of the Torah—not some of it, but every single bit. This was impossible. Furthermore, being righteous—living the Christian life—was not a result of being a good rule follower. The Christian life comes from living in faith, which boils down to being guided by the Spirit.

PROOF 3: GOD PROMISED THE SPIRIT BEFORE THE LAW EXISTED.

Brothers and sisters, I give an example from daily life: once a person's will[23] has been ratified, no one adds to it or annuls it. Now the promises were made to Abraham and to his offspring; it does not say, "And to offsprings," as of many; but it says, "And to your offspring," that is, to one person, who is Christ.

My point is this: the law, which came four hundred thirty years later, does not annul a covenant previously ratified by God, so as to nullify the promise. For if the inheritance[24] comes from the law, it no longer comes from the promise; but God granted[25] it to Abraham through the promise. (Gal 3:15–18)

Paul taught that because the law came 430 years after God had promised the Holy Spirit, the promise of the Spirit could not have been contingent on keeping the law. There was no law—no Torah and no Ten Commandments—when the promise was made to Abraham. The covenant between God and Abraham, on behalf of both Jews and gentiles, was ratified and has never been annulled. Therefore, the Holy Spirit was a gift not dependent on keeping any list of religious rules.

The rule followers disagreed with Paul. Some believed Abraham had mystically received the Torah and kept its rules, thus deserving the promise. Others believed the Torah canceled the promise and God would only be their God if they kept the rules.

Even I, who loved studying Paul's ancient letters, had grown tired of Paul's seven proofs, which were so jam packed with theology it was

23. The Greek word translated "will" does not necessarily mean a last will and testament. It means "a confirmed covenant" or "a legal agreement."

24. Inheritance includes all the benefits of being a child of God.

25. "God granted it" means "God gifted it." The promised Holy Spirit is a gift.

overwhelming. I was getting ready to start number four, but I needed to get up and move around. It was a lot to take in.

I left the cathedral and walked toward the basilica looking for my husband, wanting to express my frustration with Paul. I found my husband with a tiny white bag in his hand. In it was a sterling silver tau on a braided leather bracelet for me. It was precious and I loved it!

"All done for the day?" my husband asked.

"Yes. I'm at the part of Galatians where Paul goes on and on and on. He seems to be trying to give seven proofs to back up his theology. But he backtracks the backtracks and then repeats himself. It isn't simple repeating, he adds important concepts, but they are hard to make into one coherent direction. I stopped at number three, because number four made my head hurt. He needed an editor."

"Well that is what you do then. You assign the role of editor to your students and let them edit Paul's letter. Would be fun to see what they come up with."

"You're a tall and crafty man."

"This tall and crafty man saw a great little place to have dinner. How about a nap and then a dinner date? There must be some people we need to buy gifts for too. And maybe Paul will sound more coherent in the morning."

But after a great dinner and one more brilliant stroll through Assisi, I decided to finish Paul's last four proofs before going to bed.

PROOF 4: RELIGIOUS RULES CANNOT GIVE LIFE OR MAKE US RIGHTEOUS.

Why then the law?[26] *It was added because of transgressions, until the offspring would come to whom the promise had been made; and it was ordained through angels by a mediator. Now a mediator involves more than one party; but God is one. Is the law then opposed to the promises of God? Certainly not! For if a law had been given that could make alive, then righteousness would indeed come through the law. But the scripture has imprisoned all things under*

26. Peterson clarifies that the purpose of the law was to make obvious to everyone that we are—in ourselves—out of right relationship with God, and therefore to show us the futility of devising some religious system for getting on our own efforts what we can only get by waiting in faith for God to complete his promise. Peterson, *Traveling Light*, 98.

> the power of sin[27], so that what was promised through faith in Jesus Christ might be given to those who believe.[28]
>
> Now before faith came, we were imprisoned and guarded under the law until faith would be revealed. Therefore the law was our disciplinarian[29] until Christ came, so that we might be justified by faith. But now that faith has come, we are no longer subject to a disciplinarian.[30] (Gal 3:19–25)

The law was meant to show us our mistakes. It was not meant to save us or tell us how to live a life pleasing to God. Nor was it meant to limit our obligation to God by saying, "Do this and you're done." Furthermore, it was only needed until Jesus had completed the baptism of the Holy Spirit. This baptism of the Spirit was proclaimed by John the Baptist:

> I baptize you with water for repentance, but one who is more powerful than I is coming after me; I am not worthy to carry his sandals. He will baptize you with the Holy Spirit and fire. (Mat 3:11)

This baptism of Holy Spirit and fire took place at Pentecost:

> When the day of Pentecost had come, they were all together in one place. And suddenly from heaven there came a sound like the rush of a violent wind, and it filled the entire house where they were sitting. Divided tongues, as of fire, appeared among them, and a tongue rested on each of them. All of them were filled with the Holy Spirit. (Act 2:1–4)

Paul also wanted the Galatians to reflect upon how the Jews had received the law through a mediator, Moses.[31] God gave the law to Moses and Moses brought it to the people. But there's an issue with this. The mediator was

---

27. "The power of" is not in the Greek. It isn't the power of sin that imprisons. It is sin that imprisons.

28. Compare with Rom 11:32: "For God has imprisoned all in disobedience so that he may be merciful to all."

29. Betz points out that the word translated disciplinarian means tutor or guardian. This person was a trusted elder slave in the Roman household who was responsible for a child because the parent could not always be with them. Until the Holy Spirit came to live within us, the law gave us guidance. Betz, *Galatians*, 117.

30. We are no longer under the law, which functioned as a tutor or guardian, but have a direct relationship with God.

31. Exod 19—20.

between God and the rest of humanity. This is an inferior arrangement to having the Holy Spirit live within and guide each one of us directly.

For the Galatians, putting their faith in religious rules for guidance meant they were not dealing directly with God. Yet, God wanted a direct relationship with each of them. That was what the promise of God—to send the Spirit to live within them—was all about. The Spirit was (and is today) our direct relationship with God. The Spirit can guide us better than any set of rules. The Spirit gives us wisdom, power, and freedom. No set of rules can do that.

For me, this was Paul's most convincing argument of all. Religious rules cannot give life or make us righteous. They can't lead us to those who we need to serve, tell us where to live, or what vocation to take. They can't tell us how to live the Christian life. Only a direct relationship with God through the Holy Spirit can do that.

PROOF 5: YOU HAVE BEEN RESCUED FROM UNJUST WORLD SYSTEMS INCLUDING RELIGION.

For in Christ Jesus you are all children of God through faith.[32] *As many of you as were baptized into Christ have clothed yourselves with Christ. There is no longer Jew or Greek, there is no longer slave or free, there is no longer male and female; for all of you are one in Christ Jesus. And if you belong to Christ, then you are Abraham's offspring, heirs according to the promise.*[33] *My point is this: heirs, as long as they are minors, are no better than slaves, though they are the owners of all the property; but they remain under guardians and trustees until the date set by the father. So with us; while we were minors, we were enslaved to the elemental spirits of the world.*[34] *But when the fullness of time had come, God sent his Son, born of a woman, born under the law, in order to redeem those who were under the law, so that we might receive adoption as children. And because you are children, God has sent the Spirit of his Son into our*

32. This could be translated, "For you are all children of God through the faithfulness of Jesus."

33. Paul may have been quoting from a baptismal liturgy. He says similar things in 1 Cor 12:13 and Col 3:11.

34. Guthrie says elemental spirits are the rudiments of religion shared by non-Christians, both Jews and Gentiles. Guthrie, *Galatians*, 122.

hearts, crying, "Abba! Father!"[35] *So you are no longer a slave but a child, and if a child then also an heir, through God.*

Formerly, when you did not know God, you were enslaved to beings that by nature are not gods. Now, however, that you have come to know God, or rather to be known by God, how can you turn back again to the weak and beggarly elemental spirits? How can you want to be enslaved to them again? You are observing special days, and months, and seasons, and years.[36] *(Gal 3:26—4:10)*

Paul started by describing the Christian community as one charged with living out unprecedented social justice grounded in the belief that in Christ there is no discrimination based on race or gender. In addition, the slave and the freeperson were equal in the eyes of God. He reminded them that in this community they had been rescued from unjust world systems that discriminate against others.

Yet, because the rule followers held a very strong Jewish nationalism, they were appalled Paul was teaching that through Jesus God had adopted unclean, uncircumcised, male and female gentiles, both slave and free. Not only that, but in their adoption, Paul was teaching that these gentiles were set free from Jewish law, tradition, and discrimination. It was more than the rule followers could digest.

Furthermore, Paul also reminded the Galatians they had been rescued from the "elemental spirits"—the pagan gods, rituals, and religious rules—that they were once slaves to. Instead of living as they had in the past, now the Holy Spirit lived within them crying out *Abba,* or Father, to their creator.

"Daddy!" I said aloud. My husband and I were sitting on our rooftop porch with just a few candles lighting our table. He was reading and I was working on my laptop.

"Daddy?" asked my husband.

It touched me so deeply, I couldn't speak for a moment. "Paul wrote that the Spirit of Christ cries out to God from our hearts. And the name the Spirit calls God is *Abba,* which is what a child would have called his or her father."

35. This is a declaration that God is the father of those whom the Spirit inhabits.

36. Paul dislikes all religious rules: "You are trying to earn favor with God by observing certain days or months or seasons or years?" They were returning to the same kind of worship that they did before they knew Jesus and the Holy Spirit indwelled them.

PROOF 6: IT'S ME, PAUL!

I am afraid that my work for you may have been wasted. Friends, I beg you, become as I am, for I also have become as you are. You have done me no wrong.[37] You know that it was because of a physical infirmity that I first announced the gospel to you; though my condition put you to the test, you did not scorn or despise me, but welcomed me as an angel[38] of God, as Christ Jesus. What has become of the goodwill you felt? For I testify that, had it been possible, you would have torn out your eyes and given them to me. Have I now become your enemy by telling you the truth? They make much of you, but for no good purpose; they want to exclude you, so that you may make much of them. It is good to be made much of for a good purpose at all times, and not only when I am present with you. My little children, for whom I am again in the pain of childbirth until Christ is formed in you, I wish I were present with you now and could change my tone, for I am perplexed about you. (Gal 4:11-20)

Paul was hurt and frustrated. He was nearing the end of his seven proofs by simply reminding the Galatians that they have a history together. He had taught them the gospel. They had taken care of Paul when he was ill. They have had a good relationship. They had reason to trust him.

On the other hand, the rule followers were trying to manipulate the Galatians by alienating them from Paul, hoping the pressure would force them into becoming rule followers too. Paul is asking the question, "How can you buddy up to people who don't love you like I do?"

PROOF 7: THE LAW AND SPIRIT CANNOT EXIST TOGETHER.

Tell me, you who desire to be subject to the law, will you not listen to the law? For it is written that Abraham had two sons, one by a slave woman and the other by a free woman. One, the child of the slave, was born according to the flesh;[39] the other, the child of the

---

37. This might be better translated, "Among true friends, we cannot do each other wrong." Betz, *Galatians*, 223.

38. The word that is translated angel literally means messenger.

39. Ishmael was born according to the flesh. Abraham had grown impatient waiting

free woman, was born through the promise. Now this is an allegory: these women are two covenants. One woman, in fact, is Hagar, from Mount Sinai, bearing children for slavery. Now Hagar is Mount Sinai in Arabia and corresponds to the present Jerusalem, for she is in slavery with her children. But the other woman corresponds to the Jerusalem above; she is free, and she is our mother.

For it is written, "Rejoice, you childless one, you who bear no children, burst into song and shout, you who endure no birth pangs; for the children of the desolate woman are more numerous than the children of the one who is married."

Now you, my friends, are children of the promise, like Isaac. But just as at that time the child who was born according to the flesh persecuted the child who was born according to the Spirit, so it is now also. But what does the scripture say? "Drive out the slave and her child; for the child of the slave will not share[40] *the inheritance with the child of the free woman."*[41] *So then, friends, we are children, not of the slave but of the free woman. (Gal 4:21–31)*

Abraham, who was eighty-seven years old, and Sarah, who was seventy-six years old, had a choice. Either trust God by waiting for their promised child through whom Jesus would descend, or help God out by using Hagar, their slave, as a surrogate. Trusting God would mean the child would be born of the free woman, Sarah. Not trusting God would mean the child was born of the slave, Hagar.

They made the choice to take matters into their own hands. Hagar conceived a child named Ishmael. He represents the law. But later Sarah, the freewoman, conceived a child named Isaac. Isaac represents the promise of the Spirit.

The law and the Spirit cannot exist together. Therefore, Abraham eventually drove Ishmael and Hagar away to protect the child born of the promise. Paul was telling the Galatians that to protect their freedom they must drive out the rule followers from their community.

In addition, Paul called the Galatians "children of the promise." This would have infuriated the rule followers who thought the Jews were the children of the promise. But the rule followers have excluded themselves

for God to bring about Sarah's promised pregnancy. So Abraham took matters into his own hands and had sex with his slave.

40. Not sharing the inheritance means that the Galatians will have to choose between law and Spirit. They don't mix.

41. Gen 21:10.

from grace and from the guidance of the Spirit. They placed themselves in bondage under the curse of the law.

If we try to live the Christian life by keeping both Ishmael and Isaac—both the law and the Spirit—they will spin us in circles. We will sink into rule following whenever we do not have the desire or will to wait upon the Holy Spirit. We will live in slavery rather than freedom.

"That's it! Done for the night!" I exclaimed.

"That was fast! Sounds like Paul's last arguments weren't as complex as the first ones."

"No, but number seven really bothers me. I get what Paul was saying, but to compare an innocent child to the law is disturbing on so many levels. Then to make matters worse, Abraham ran him off because he no longer wanted him after his wife conceived and bore the promised child. That is disgusting."

"What?"

"Abraham didn't wait patiently for God to give him an heir. So he had a child through a slave. Bad enough right?"

"I'd say so."

"Then after Ishmael, the son of the slave, is born, Abraham's wife, Sarah, gives birth to the child God promised."

"That was Isaac?"

"Yes, but then Abraham runs Ishmael and his mother, Hagar, off. It's horrible. I don't like Abraham very much."

"Well, not much about him to like in that story."

"In the story, God does look out for Ishmael and his mother, but Abraham and Sarah were horrible. I am mad at them."

"All because they took matters into their own hands instead of waiting for God?

"When you put it that way. Best we wait for God to speak to us."

The air had turned chilly and I was longing to go inside to sleep.

Spiritual Practice 3
Inflamed by the Spirit

THIS FINAL SECTION OF "A Letter to the Entire Order" was written by Francis shortly before his death. At this point, Francis was very upset at the direction the order was taking, because they were embracing less and less of the severe poverty required by Francis. However, this beautiful prayer is how he ends the letter.

PRAYER FOR THE ORDER[1]

Almighty, eternal, just, and merciful God, grant us in our misery the grace to do for you alone what we know you want us to do, and always to desire what pleases you. Thus, inwardly cleansed, interiorly enlightened, and inflamed by the fire of the Holy Spirit, may we be able to follow in the footprints of your beloved son, our Lord Jesus Christ. And, by your grace alone, may we make our way to you, Most High, who live and rule in perfect trinity and simple unity, and are glorified God all-powerful forever and ever. Amen.

STEP 1

Find a quiet place to pray.

STEP 2

Pray the *Prayer for the Order*. Pray it slowly thinking over each word.

1. St. Francis, *Francis of Assisi: Early Documents, Vol. 1, The Saint*, 120.

Step 3

Meditate on finding the desire to obey the Holy Spirit. During your meditation, return to the prayer as needed. Journal your thoughts.

PART 4

The Way Forward

10

How Do We Live the Christian Life?
Galatians 5:1—6:10

THE NEXT MORNING WE slept in late, missing the breakfast part of our bed and breakfast. Therefore, we went looking among the ancient stone buildings for a *mercato* to buy a loaf of bread and two freshly squeezed orange juices. Our plan was to eat our picnic breakfast in the Piazza del Comune, which we did sitting on the steps of the Chiesa di Santa Maria sopra Minerva and watching as the people of Assisi went on about their daily business.

I had not encountered the Church of St. Maria in any of my research about Francis. That was because it had changed functions and religions over the years. It began as a Roman temple, Tempo di Minerva, to the goddess Minerva—a goddess of wisdom and warfare.[1] This was no surprise with its six Romanesque columns holding up a roof that shaded a typical temple porch. During Francis's lifetime, the building was a prison and later the headquarters of the *magistrato,* or local court. Although today the Church of St. Maria sits squeezed between other more recent buildings, it originally sat alone, raised above the ground with double the number of steps leading up to it. We enjoyed a tour of the church, although the baroque interior was a complete surprise and seemed disjointed with the rest of Assisi.

---

1. Recent archeologists theorize that the temple may have been connected with the Castor and Pollux cult rather than Minerva.

Assisi was a ghost town this morning compared to the lively town that had been flooded by Italian crowds for the *Festa di San Francesco d'Assisi* and then the day after for the *Fiera di San Francesco*. It almost felt lonely, probably because we both knew our pilgrimage was coming to a close and we would inevitably have to leave this mystical place. The question we had asked many times a day, "How do we live the Christian Life?" was still not completely answered. We had learned the following:

- The Christian life was lived by being faithful to the faithfulness of Christ.
- The Christian life was lived by following the Holy Spirit rather than a set of religious rules.

We had started the pilgrimage thinking we were looking for answers more specific to our circumstances. Perhaps God might tell us to foster a child, me to write another book, my husband to take a job in another state, or us to become part of a parachurch living and working inside a community in the impoverished parts of a big city. Instead, we were learning how to seek these answers. Instead of giving us answers, God was showing us how to ask for and how to hear the answers.

We suspected being "faithful as Christ had been faithful" meant we needed the desire to carry God's directions through. We knew we couldn't manufacture it on our own. There were some obvious places to seek answers, like studying scripture, but honestly so much of the study of scripture had just led to more rule making, endless debates over theology, but not to living out the Christian life with integrity. At any rate, we still had questions.

We had not yet been to the Basilica di Santa Chiara where the actual cross that spoke to Francis in the San Damiano Church now hung. Having saved our visit there for the very end of our pilgrimage, we decided it was time.[2]

"Has the cross ever spoken to anyone else?" asked my husband.

"Not that I know of, but maybe it will speak to you!" I teased. And off we went.

In Francis's day, the land where the Basilica of St. Clare now sits was just outside of the city gate. Today the *piazza* in front of the basilica is more like an oversize terrace than a village square. It offers a magnificent view of the valley below, as well as a view upward of Rocca Maggiore looming over

2. See picture 36 in the appendix.

Assisi. Standing in the *piazza* in front of the basilica, one can see where the original building with a brick façade ended and was then extended (with blocks of stone in alternating colors of pink and white) to become the cathedral. The original building, known as the Cappella di San Giorgio, once held both a hospital and the school that the young Francis attended. The magnificent cathedral now houses the remains of Clare and her sister Agnes.

Clare had been born into a noble Assisi family and made the decision at sixteen to follow Francis into a life of service and poverty, eventually becoming the Abbess of San Damiano. She was the first woman to follow Francis. However, her running away from home to the Porziuncola during Holy Week was not greeted with shouts of joy from her family, nor was her younger sister Agnes's departure a week later. Even though Clare convinced her father to let her stay, the father dragged Agnes away through the fields until her body mysteriously became so heavy that the gang of relatives with him could no longer lift her. When the relatives abandoned Agnes and fled in fear, Clare retrieved her sister. Clare would continue to lead the order of the Poor Clares for many years even after Francis's death. During that time, she watched on in dismay as the Franciscans strayed further and further away from Francis's vision.

We entered the main doors of the cathedral expecting the San Damiano cross to be front and center over the altar. Yet, the byzantine cross that hung there was not the cross that had spoken to Francis. Confused, we turned to our right into the Chapel of St. George where we found it hanging from a most unusual asymmetrical ceiling.[3] And there Giovanni was, kneeling at the altar beneath the cross, praying. We bowed reverencing the cross, approached it, and knelt next to him.

My husband and I, both in our own way, spoke to God silently, asking the question again, "How do we live the Christian life?" We lost track of time as we prayed. I meditated on the last six weeks. My mind went place to place considering all the things we had experienced—the weeks on the Cammino di Assisi going from churches to monasteries, the weeks at the *agriturismo*, and now this time in Assisi. It was a pilgrimage of a lifetime in which the Italian countryside had stood lovingly in all its glory around us. We felt embraced by it.

After some time, I felt someone lightly touch my shoulder. Giovanni stood between and behind my husband and me. With his hands placed on

---

3. See picture 37 in the appendix.

both of our shoulders, he leaned down and whispered, "I must leave, but I will be in the *piazza* out front later in the morning."

We smiled and thanked him. The last we had seen him, he had said he couldn't tell us how to live the Christian life, but he could tell us how to find out. We had many questions to ask him.

We knelt in front of the cross for a while longer. The Poor Clares who were praying thinned out until we were alone. Together in a whisper, just as we had done in San Damiano, we prayed the prayer Francis had humbly and earnestly prayed in front of this cross centuries before.[4]

In a sense, Francis had been asking the same question we had. When we were done, we walked out to the *piazza* and sat at the far end near the statue of a rather kindly looking gold lion.

My husband said what we were both thinking, "If I were to summarize all we have learned over the last six weeks, I would say we must figure out how to be in sync with the wisdom and power of the Holy Spirit. Because writing a rule of life or adopting the rule of life of a community—if it is nothing more than a fixed set of religious rules—is clearly not the way for us."

"I agree that is what Paul taught."

"It sounds as if you aren't sure you agree with Paul."

"Two things. First, I think we agree not all rules of life followed by those who have taken Holy Orders are truly rules—some are what I would call wisdom guidelines." My husband shook his head in agreement. "Secondly, I do think Paul is right. What he teaches makes sense to me—not just logically, but it makes sense from a historical perspective."

"You mean it is what the ancient prophets prophesied?"

"Yes—it makes the Old Testament and New Testament work together. But . . . " I paused thinking it over. "I look at the amazing life Francis led and I don't want to degrade him or his spirituality in any way. He desired to serve God with all he was. That is simply amazing. Service to God led him to serve others and creation with all he could muster. He is still having an effect on the world today."

"He got a lot right."

"That is what Giovanni said when we first met him."

"Francis got a lot right, but not everything," my husband said, repeating in entirety what Giovanni had said. "Jesus gets everything right, so neither we nor Francis have to."

4. This prayer can be found in Spiritual Practice 2 in this book.

"Exactly!" I smiled at my husband. "It hurts me that Francis didn't understand that God didn't require—or even desire—the self-loathing and punishment he took on. Instead of throwing himself into rose bushes and ditches or going without sleep and food as penitence, I want him to have taken better care of himself. He might have lived a lot longer and had an even bigger legacy—if that is possible."

"He might not have lost control of his order either. Maybe he would have been a stronger administrator."

We looked over the valley below Assisi, feeling content. I could imagine Francis walking through those fields—such a complex man, full of joy and depression all at once, but always such a desire to love God.

Then my husband asked again, "So how do we live the Christian life?"

"Serendipitously, I think the answer is found in the final chapters of Galatians. Do you want to see what I'm talking about?"

Over the next set of verses, Paul described the Christian life using several different phrases: living *through* the Spirit, living *by* the Spirit, living by the Spirit's *desires, led* by the Spirit, *producing the fruit* of the Spirit, *guided* by the Spirit, *receiving* the Spirit, and *sowing* to the Spirit. Paul was describing something brand new in the world and it was as if he hadn't settled on the best vocabulary for this concept yet. Or maybe Paul was simply capturing the fact the Spirit works in many different ways. Jesus described the Spirit's work like this:

> The wind blows where it chooses, and you hear the sound of it,
> but you do not know where it comes from or where it goes. So it is
> with everyone who is born of the Spirit. (John 3:8)

I took a deep breath. "I have come to believe the Christian life is ultimately lived by letting the wisdom of the Spirit guide us and the power of the Spirit empower us."

"So being faithful to the faithfulness of Christ is done by letting the wisdom of the Spirit—the same Spirit who guided Christ—guide us. And by letting the power of the Spirit—not our own power—empower us to do the work of God," summarized my husband.

"Yes. And in chapter 5 of Galatians, in what I have come to believe are some of the most important verses in the Bible, Paul delves into five lessons that describe life lived in the Spirit."

LESSON 1: LIFE IN THE SPIRIT IS LIVED IN FREEDOM.

> *For freedom Christ has set us free. Stand firm, therefore, and do not submit again to a yoke of slavery. Listen! I, Paul, am telling you that if you let yourselves be circumcised, Christ will be of no benefit to you. Once again I testify to every man who lets himself be circumcised that he is obliged to obey the entire law. You who want to be justified by the law have cut yourselves off from Christ; you have fallen away from grace. (Gal 5:1–4)*

I suspected many modern Christians, if they really thought about it, would throw up their hands here in disbelief. For a long time in America, we have been defining our denominations by which set of religious rules we follow. We have been afraid to let others have the privilege of hearing God speak directly to them. Instead, we suck the life out of the Spirit by insisting we all agree on the religious rules. In other words, we classify each other by which rules we keep. Clergy have spent a lot of time teaching their list of rules, but not teaching their congregations how to live in the Spirit.

The Galatians, once set free from their pagan religious rules, were now leaning toward returning to slavery by adopting the Jewish religious rules. Like those who have spent a long time incarcerated, the Galatians wanted the safety of the prison walls again. This was a theme in scripture particularly well emphasized in the Exodus story.[5] After God brought the ancient Jews out of slavery in Egypt, God dwelled in a cloud at the edge of their campsite. The cloud would move to guide them where God wanted them to go. But instead of following God, they wanted to return to Egypt where they would be slaves again. The Israelites did not like their freedom, because it was too scary to rely on God's daily guidance. They felt safer and more in control of their lives when they had been slaves.

After we had talked through this portion of Galatians, I turned to my husband and said, "Following the Spirit, obeying the Spirit, being mindful that the Spirit is with us and active in our lives, is the only way to live the Christian life."

"So did Francis obey the Spirit?"

"Yes and no. He had more of a desire to obey God than anyone I've ever heard of! He was genuine to the core. And he spontaneously turned to the Spirit for guidance all the time. However, when it came to his list of

---

5. Exod 13:21.

rules, he became uncompromising and blind to the thought that the Holy Spirit might want to work outside the boundaries of poverty Francis had set for God."

"He set the rule of poverty, not God?"

"I think so. I have been thinking it was his reaction to the baggage from a father who tried to manipulate him with material things. He took the words spoken by Jesus as words meant to transcend time and space."

Just then, a shadow fell upon my notebook. We looked up to see Giovanni standing between us and the sun.

"You are right about Francis and the Spirit," Giovanni said with his big smile. "Let me tell you a story."

Like always, Giovanni half told and half acted out his stories. Rather than sit next to us, he continued to stand in front of us so he had our entire attention. Fortunately for us, the sun passed behind a thick cloud so we didn't go blind as we watched him.

"As most people are aware," began Giovanni with flamboyant gestures toward the few unsuspecting people mulling around us in the square, "Francis had a great love for nature, because a loving God had created it and placed God's love within it. One day Francis found himself inside the turreted walls of the fortress town of Alviano facing down a flock of birds." Stepping out of storytelling mode, he added, "Even today, Alviano is an oasis for birds with over 150 species migrating there each year."

"Really?" asked my husband, half-teasing Giovanni for the energy he was putting into his story. Meanwhile, pigeons had descended on the fountain behind Giovanni. They were bathing happily in the sparkling water.

Giovanni waved toward them making sure we noticed them, "Birds always show up when I tell this story!" he smiled. Birds were always all over the fountains in Assisi, so again my husband and I had to try hard to keep a straight face. Nevertheless, Giovanni playfully ignored us and went on, "Francis had come to Alviano to teach the gospel of poverty and of service, but there were so many nesting swallows that the people who'd gathered in the central *piazza* couldn't hear Francis over the shrieking." Giovanni stopped, then bent to our eye level, and asked us, "Do you think Francis took this as a sign he was to stop preaching?"

My husband and I both laughed aloud this time at his flair for the dramatic and spontaneously leaned back slightly, making room for more personal space between us and Giovanni. Then we looked at each other, and I answered, "My guess is . . ." then with gusto and upward arm movements to match that of Giovanni, "Of course not!"

"No, of course not!" responded Giovanni, pleased I was playing along with his drama. "Francis simply turned to the birds and said, 'Sisters, you have said enough. Let me speak.'" The pigeons behind us at the sound of Giovanni's booming voice flew away to sit on the *piazza* wall.

"The birds flew away when Francis yelled at them?" teased my husband.

"No! Francis did not yell. The birds became quiet when Francis spoke gently to them!" Giovanni was not at all put off at our laughter and teasing. He enjoyed it and went on, "The people were so astonished that they wanted to follow Francis wherever he would lead them. The entire city immediately decided to abandon Alviano and follow Francis that very day. Obviously, this created quite a problem for Francis. How could whole families with babies and children live in the abject poverty he required of those in his order? Mothers and children could not live under bridges or beg for food at every meal."

"Good point!" I said aloud and gestured with my hand toward my husband as if to say listen up. "So Giovanni, how did Francis solve the problem of how families were to live the Christian life?"

"He told them he would go away. By himself. And pray. Then he would return with an answer as to what they should do 'for the salvation of their souls.'"[6]

"So he sought the wisdom of the Spirit when his rules didn't work for him!" I said as I looked at my husband. "You see . . . he and Paul were living more on the same page than one would think!"

Then to Giovanni, I asked, "Did Francis keep his word? Did he return with an answer as to how they were to live the Christian life?"

Giovanni hemmed and hawed as if he didn't want to answer my question. Eventually he cracked a hearty grin and said, "The point is Francis went and sought the guidance of the Spirit."

Seeing he wished he could give me a tidy answer, I lightheartedly demanded, "Answer my question Giovanni!"

"Okay. Sadly, he returned with a new set of rules."

"Oh no!" I declared.

"Wait." Giovanni cautioned, "The rule of life for families and lay people was a much more relaxed set of rules—really more a set of guidelines

---

6. Celano, *The Francis Trilogy*, 300–301.

than hard and fast rules. Fortunately, the families who became the lay order of Franciscans would not be required to live in poverty, but to live simply instead. And serving others was still very much at the heart of their lives."

Giovanni sat down in front of me cross-legged on the ground, carefully pulling his skirt discreetly over his ankles. "The important thing is . . . what would *you* have told them?"

"What would I have told the families of Alviano? Because of my recent studies, I have a different answer than I would have had last week. Last week, I would have given them the best set of rules I could provide. But now I would teach them how to seek the Spirit's guidance for themselves. I would equip them with the knowledge that God wants to speak directly to them."

"You would have taught them how to ask, seek, and knock on God's door.[7] I thought you didn't know how to live the Christian Life?" whispered Giovanni quietly. "You—actually the Holy Spirit—have answered your pilgrimage question."

"But how do we do that?" asked my husband, "How do we seek and knock?"

"Oh, there's no formula with the Spirit. You prayed the prayer of Francis in front of the cross, did you not? You went on this pilgrimage. You continue doing this with each of life's specific questions. You pray and then you wait patiently and listen. God may answer while you pray, speaking into your free flowing thoughts. Or God may wait many days and show up in the words of a complete stranger. But because you're looking for the Holy Spirit, you'll see the wind blowing in the trees when the Holy Spirit speaks. You will know."

Giovanni stopped and looked into the tree under which the statue of the lion sat. He paused and waited. And waited. But no wind blew through the trees. There was no rustling of leaves. Then he chuckled, "Now if Francis had just said that, there would have been a sudden gentle wind!" He waited another moment and a breeze came. "There!" he said.

My husband and I gave him looks of "Really?" And again he laughed and went on, "The difference between us and Francis is we have his experience to learn from. Be aware of that baggage you were just speaking of. It can become a hindrance for you to hear the Spirit. This is another of Francis's gifts to you! Baggage can make you think you know right and wrong when you don't. Keep praying that prayer. Keep reading Paul's letter. And

7. Matt 7:7.

most importantly keep seeking God's answers." And with that Giovanni danced down the street with no good-bye.

When he was out of eyesight, as if nothing unusual at all had just happened, my husband said, "Let's go somewhere and get some gelato."

"Okay! Why not? Do you think we will see him again?" I said looking toward the way Giovani had gone, through the gigantic flying buttresses that held up the cathedral.

"I don't think we could avoid him if we tried. He'll find us. Still hoping he doesn't show up in our shower one morning."

"There are just two mornings left. The day after tomorrow we take the train back to Rome."

"I know."

LESSON 2: LIFE IN THE SPIRIT IS LIVED BY FAITH WORKING THROUGH LOVE.

For through the Spirit, by faith, we eagerly wait for the hope of righteousness. For in Christ Jesus neither circumcision nor uncircumcision counts for anything; the only thing that counts is faith working through love. You were running well[8]; who prevented you from obeying the truth? Such persuasion does not come from the one who calls you. A little yeast leavens the whole batch of dough. I am confident about you in the Lord that you will not think otherwise. But whoever it is that is confusing you will pay the penalty. But my friends, why am I still being persecuted if I am still preaching circumcision?[9] In that case the offense of the cross has been removed. I wish those who unsettle you would castrate themselves![10] (Gal 5:5–12)

The hope of righteousness was the hope that one day we would do better than getting a lot of things right. The hope was that we would get it all right. Not just individually, but the whole community of faith—in fact, the whole

8. A better translation might be "You were running correctly."

9. Apparently, there was an attempt by the rule followers to convince the Galatians that Paul was now teaching that they should be circumcised.

10. It takes a bit of imagination to think Paul was suggesting that they castrate themselves. The word for castration is simply not there in the Greek. More likely, Paul is wishing those who are upsetting the Galatians would cut themselves off from the community. Young's Literal Translation gets it right, "O that even they would cut themselves off who are unsettling you!"

world—would get it all right. This is what we prayed for in church every time we prayed the Lord's Prayer, "Thy Kingdom come, thy will be done." That is what my husband and I longed for. Francis had desired this too—in spades.

In addition, life in the Spirit is lived with a faith that works through love. This kind of love is not only the end of rule following because it fulfills the intention of all worthwhile rules—but it puts into clear focus when rules should be bent and broken too.

> One Sabbath Jesus was going through the grain fields; and as they made their way his disciples began to pluck heads of grain. The *rule following*[11] Pharisees said to him, "Look, why are they doing what is not lawful on the Sabbath?" And he said to them, "Have you never read what David did when he and his companions were hungry and in need of food? He entered the house of God, when Abiathar was high priest, and ate the bread of the Presence, which it is not lawful for any but the priests to eat, and he gave some to his companions." Then he said to them, "The Sabbath was made for humankind, and not humankind for the Sabbath; so the Son of Man is lord even of the Sabbath." Again Jesus entered the synagogue, and a man was there who had a withered hand. The Pharisees watched him to see whether he would cure him on the Sabbath, so that they might accuse him.[12] And he said to the man who had the withered hand, "Come forward." Then he said to them, "Is it lawful to do good or to do harm on the Sabbath, to save life or to kill?" But they were silent. He looked around at them with anger; he was grieved at their hardness of heart and said to the man, "Stretch out your hand." He stretched it out, and his hand was restored. The Pharisees went out and immediately conspired with the Herodians against him, how to destroy him. (Mark 3:1–6)

Living with a faith that works through love also puts into clear focus when God is calling us to go far beyond the rules to love others. Love can get complicated. Sometimes it needs to be tough and other times it needs to be gentle. The Holy Spirit will guide us. Jesus knew when it was okay to break the law, because the Holy Spirit guided him. He knew healing a man on the Sabbath was an act of faith based on love.

11. "Rule following" has been added by the author for effect and is not in the scripture.

12. Curing someone on the Sabbath was considered work by the rule following Pharisees. Work was not allowed on the Sabbath.

LESSON 3: LIFE IN THE SPIRIT IS NOT SELF-INDULGENT.

For you were called to freedom, brothers and sisters; only do not use your freedom as an opportunity for self-indulgence, but through love become slaves to one another. For the whole law is summed up in a single commandment, "You shall love your neighbor as yourself." If, however, you bite and devour one another, take care that you are not consumed by one another.

Live by the Spirit, I say, and do not gratify the desires of the flesh. For what the flesh desires is opposed to the Spirit, and what the Spirit desires is opposed to the flesh; for these are opposed to each other, to prevent you from doing what you want. But if you are led by the Spirit, you are not subject to the law. (Gal 5:13–18)

Paul was redefining the Jewish understanding of sin. For Paul, sin was two-fold—it was both "the works of the law" and "the works of the flesh." He defined the works of the law as trying to keep the law—or do anything at all—in order to earn God's love and blessings. The Galatians could not (nor can we) control God's love and blessings, because God gave (gives) them freely. Paul defined the works of the flesh as trying to satisfy self at the cost of loving and serving others. Engaging in either the works of the law or the works of the flesh was the opposite of living the Christian life.

Paul wanted the Galatians to live in freedom, but he recognized there was a danger in being free. Freedom could be used for selfishness. However, by relying on the Holy Spirit, he taught that the Galatians would defeat selfishness. I had jotted down a quote from one of the scholars whose work I been studying:

> If the human subject allows the Spirit to completely influence and fill out his (or her) life then the opposite force, the intentions of the flesh, will be prevented from accomplishing their goal, so that the 'works of the flesh' cannot happen.[13]

By loving others to the point of becoming slaves to them—by truly putting their needs before one's own needs—we are living in the Spirit. For certain, life in the Spirit is not lived by being self-indulgent or by doing things that would hurt others.

13. Betz, *Galatians*, 278.

LESSON 4: LIFE IN THE SPIRIT IS EMPOWERED BY THE HOLY SPIRIT.

> *Now the works of the flesh are obvious: fornication, impurity, licentiousness, idolatry, sorcery, enmities, strife, jealousy, anger, quarrels, dissensions, factions, envy, drunkenness, carousing, and things like these. I am warning you, as I warned you before: those who do such things will not inherit the kingdom of God. By contrast, the fruit of the Spirit is love, joy, peace, patience, kindness, generosity, faithfulness, gentleness, and self-control. There is no law against such things. And those who belong to Christ Jesus have crucified the flesh with its passions and desires. (Gal 5:19–24)*

Paul made two lists, one of the works of the flesh and one of the fruit of the Spirit. Works are what we do on our own. Fruit is what happens spontaneously as a result of the Spirit living within us.

An apple tree doesn't need an instruction manual to produce fruit. It is spontaneous. Likewise, the fruit of the Spirit is spontaneous. We don't have to work at it. It happens because of who we become as the Spirit transforms us. One thing is for sure, apple trees do best when they are nurtured with rain, sun, and good soil. In the next section of verses, Paul called this kind of nurturing "sowing to the Spirit." We can tend to our fruit tree by making sure it is exposed to the things that help produce fruit. But the empowerment to produce fruit (to be righteous, to live the Christian life, to follow Jesus) comes from the Spirit.

I also noted the fruit of the Spirit was singular. The fruit was love and all the other descriptive words (joy, peace, patience, kindness, generosity, faithfulness, gentleness, and self-control) were what developed as a result of love. Unlike the gifts of the Spirit, where we each have varied and different gifts, we should *all* produce the fruit of the Spirit.[14]

LESSON 5: LIFE IN THE SPIRIT SOWS TO THE SPIRIT.

> *If we live by the Spirit, let us also be guided by the Spirit.[15] Let us not become conceited, competing against one another, envying one*

14. 1 Cor 12:4–12.

15. A better translation might be, "If the Spirit is our source of life, let us also be

> another. *My friends, if anyone is detected in a transgression, you who have received the Spirit should restore such a one in a spirit of gentleness. Take care that you yourselves are not tempted. Bear one another's burdens, and in this way you will fulfill the law of Christ.*
>
> *For if those who are nothing think they are something, they deceive themselves. All must test their own work; then that work, rather than their neighbor's work, will become a cause for pride. For all must carry their own loads.*[16] *Those who are taught the word must share in all good things with their teacher. Do not be deceived; God is not mocked, for you reap whatever you sow.*
>
> *If you sow to your own flesh, you will reap corruption from the flesh; but if you sow to the Spirit, you will reap eternal life from the Spirit. So let us not grow weary in doing what is right, for we will reap at harvest time, if we do not give up. So then, whenever we have an opportunity, let us work for the good of all, and especially for those of the family of faith. (Gal 5:25—6:10)*

Paul taught the Galatians that their freedom should not be used to separate themselves from others, but to build up both the church and the world. They were to live a shared life.[17] They were not independent, but interdependent. Paul gave them some examples of how the family of faith—the church—should treat one another when the Spirit is guiding them. These are common sense reminders all summed up by loving one another. It was possible these specific examples are ones Paul had heard were a problem in the Galatian church.

It seems contradictory to all Paul had said previously, but in these verses Paul talked about fulfilling the "law of Christ." Some theologians have taken this to mean Jesus replaced the Torah with his own law. To figure out what the law of Christ was, they have gone through the New Testament looking for rules to follow. But the law of Christ was to love one another with a love that is guided by the Spirit.[18,19] Irenaeus, one of

---

guided by the Spirit."

16. "All must carry their own loads" has sometimes been misinterpreted to mean that all loads should be equal. It doesn't say that. Whatever load God has given us to carry, we carry it. In addition, we help carry the loads of others.

17. "Let us work for the good of all." Gal 6:10.

18. John 13:34 and 15:12.

19. Hawthorne writes, "The context of the 'law of Christ' is set within walking in, being guided by, and sowing to the Spirit." Hawthorne, *Dictionary of Paul and His Letters*, 544.

the early Christian fathers wrote, "Jesus became what we are so we might become what he is."[20] In other words, the law of Christ was to love like Jesus and that can only be done through the Holy Spirit.

Finally, the Galatians were to live the Christian life by sowing to the Spirit. The Galatians' relationship to the Spirit was not passive. Although the Spirit was a free gift, their part was to sow. Sowing determined one's basic direction in life. They could sow self-indulgently and reap a life that was destructive to others and themselves, or they could nurture the things of the Spirit.

In one of the commentaries I studied, Wiersbe wrote that all of our resources (material possessions, skills, ability to act and work, to vote, etc.) are seed. Then he explained there are two kinds of soil where we can plant this seed: Flesh and Spirit.[21] Thomas Aquinas wrote sowing to the Spirit meant a person "directs his (or her) interest to the service of the Spirit by serving justice through faith and love."[22] The early church sowed to the Spirit by devoting themselves to the study of scripture, fellowship, and prayer.[23]

In the end, Paul seemed to be prioritizing the family of faith over all others: "especially for those of the family of faith." This may be off-putting and seem exclusive, but this is necessary. Taking care of the family of faith must happen so we can take care of others together.[24]

20. Bettenson, *The Early Christian Fathers*, 351.

21. Wiersbe, *Be Free*, 146,

22. Aquinas, *Commentary on the Letters of St. Paul to the Galatians*, un-paginated document, Chapter 6 Lecture 2.

23. Acts 2:42.

24. Barclay, *Obeying the Truth*, 166.

11

What Really Matters
Galatians 6:11–18

OUR SECOND TO LAST night in Assisi we slept like babies. We had no real plans for the day except to stroll through the streets of Assisi, take as many pictures as possible, visit our favorite churches, eat some great Italian food, buy a few trinkets, and drink some memorable wine. We simply wanted to soak it all up one last time. Tomorrow morning we would catch a taxi to the train that would take us to Rome for our flight home to Atlanta.

No longer surprised by Giovanni showing up anywhere and at any time, we weren't especially surprised to find a simple handwritten invitation waiting for us on the kitchen table of our bed and breakfast. Giovanni was inviting us to a special Mass that night which would take place in the Porziuncola, the tiny chapel housed within the Basilica di Santa Maria degli Angeli. The invitation said a new *ricordiamo* would be commissioned at the service.

I turned to my husband to ask what a *ricordiamo* was.

"Literally it means 'we remember.' Other than that, I have no idea. But this sounds like something we do not want to miss."

"Agreed!"

I showed the invitation to the owner of the bed and breakfast, asking if she knew what this was all about. She didn't. "What does it matter?" was her reply. "You can't say no to Giovanni."

True. Nor did we want to say no. We were certain it would be something special.

We arranged to take a taxi down the hill into the valley that night so we'd look presentable when we got there. But for now, we began a day of meandering. As usual, after a while my husband asked, "So where are we in Galatians?"

"At the end!" I exclaimed happily. "I am going to be ready to teach my class now."

At the end of the epistle, Paul takes over from the person to whom he was dictating the letter and begins to write the ending himself. He comments that his handwriting is so large. And then he begins to shame the rule followers.

See what large letters I make when I am writing in my own hand! It is those who want to make a good showing in the flesh that try to compel you to be circumcised—only that they may not be persecuted for the cross of Christ. Even the circumcised do not themselves obey the law, but they want you to be circumcised so that they may boast about your flesh. May I never boast of anything except the cross of our Lord Jesus Christ, by which the world has been crucified to me, and I to the world.[1] *(Gal 6:11–14)*

"Why was his handwriting so bad?" asked my husband.

"He doesn't say. Maybe because his vision was bad? Maybe because he had been beaten so many times he didn't have full use of his hands? He doesn't dwell on it long, but rapidly moves toward accusing the rule followers of trying to avoid persecution."

"Persecution?"

"Non-Christian Jews wanted the Jewish Christians out of the synagogues and temple, not because the Jewish Christians believed Jesus was the Messiah, but because Jewish Christians were opening the doors of these holy places to unclean and uncircumcised gentiles. So Paul was accusing the rule followers of demanding circumcision because they wanted to avoid persecution. Being forced to leave the place where one has worshiped God

---

1. In other words, Paul no longer participated in unjust world systems including religions that sought to enslave others with a list of rules. He no longer tried to fit in.

and where one's ancestors have worshiped God was understandably distressing. If the gentiles converted to Judaism, then, in theory, they would no longer be outcasts. Paul, however, declares he is above worrying about such persecution. Then . . ."

I paused as a small boy took pictures of his parents with a toy camera in front of a stuffed wild boar's head outside of an Assisi deli. They held a leash with a friendly French bulldog on the other end. We stopped to pet the dog while the child took pictures of us too.

As we walked away, my husband whispered, "What do you think they tell the kid when he gets home and wants to see the photos he took?"

"Good question!"

I went on not quite remembering where I was, "Well, this last part of the letter makes it clear that though Paul and Francis would have disagreed about religious rules, they also had a lot in common. They both suffered physically from illnesses. They were both "branded" with the marks of Christ. Both thought boasting was wrong because their entire lives should point to God. Neither was afraid of being persecuted. Both were authentic and disliked by many people who weren't. And both rejected world systems. Paul rejected the Jewish religious law and cultural norms, including laws regarding race and gender. Francis rejected the economic system—the use of money along with every kind of materialism. Neither was interested in pursuing the goals of the world."

"But most of all, they both had this insatiable desire to give everything they were to God," concluded my husband.

"So true. Desire to do the work of God defined them more than anything else."

"Do you think Francis ever doubted his choices?"

"He did actually. After he had been pushed out of his role as the leader of the Franciscans, he went to see a few brothers who had made a little structure for him to sleep in. Weariness and regret had laid hold of him and not only was he hearing voices, but he had come to doubt his choices. In the middle of a sleepless night, a vision of what might have been—a happy home with a wife and children—entered his mind."

"Let me guess, he found a ditch with rose bushes and threw himself into it?"

"He pretty much hurt himself until he actually bled, but the vision of his would-be family would not leave him. So he ran from the cabin into the snow naked. There he built a wife and then children out of snow. He grieved greatly over what might have been. But it was when he realized he would need to also build snowman servants to carry all of his family's belongings that he finally realized he had made the right choice. Once again joyful, he returned to the arms of Lady Poverty."[2]

"Then?" my husband prompted.

"Then?"

"Back when we saw the boy with the toy camera, you were saying 'Paul then . . .' but were distracted by the boy. I got the feeling Paul does something in the last verses that is important."

"Oh yeah. *Then* Paul finishes with a statement he should have started with."

For neither circumcision nor uncircumcision is anything; but a new creation is everything! As for those who will follow this rule[3]— peace be upon them, and mercy, and upon the Israel of God.[4] From now on, let no one make trouble for me; for I carry the marks of Jesus branded on my body. May the grace of our Lord Jesus Christ be with your spirit, brothers and sisters. Amen. (Gal 6:15–18)

"What? Circumcision doesn't matter?" my husband asked. "So after all that he says it doesn't matter whether you're circumcised or not? Give me a break."

"I know! But what he means is circumcision is a symbol. The act itself is neither here nor there. It is what it signifies that is important. Those who agree to follow the law, instead of allowing the Spirit to transform them into the new creation, have missed out on experiencing God's grace and freedom."

"Am I missing something? Has Paul talked about this new creation before?'

"Yes and no. This is the only time he uses the "new creation" vocabulary in the Epistle to the Galatians, but it is what he has been describing all along. We are the new creation. We are no longer our old selves; we are now joined with the Spirit who is transforming us. We are a new race of people with the Spirit's DNA implanted into our own. This new creation is

---

2. Chalippe, *The Life and Legends of Saint Francis of Assisi*, 330.

3. Paul loved sarcasm. Calling what he had been teaching them "a rule" was typical Paul sarcasm.

4. Israel only included Jews by birth. Israel of God included gentile Christians, not just those who were Jewish by birth.

free to live in the guidance of the Spirit. We are not to return to a long list of rules to follow, to the unyielding search for a perfect theology, or to a list of good works that must be done. We now produce the fruit of the Spirit, which all begins and ends in love for God and others. Paul talks about this new creation when he writes to the Corinthians, "So if anyone is in Christ, there is a new creation: everything old has passed away; see, everything has become new!" (2 Cor 5:17).

"This new creation is the whole point of Paul's letter," my husband pondered.

"It is the whole point of Jesus's death and resurrection which enabled the sending of the Spirit—the day of Pentecost. It is how we are able to participate in the mission of God."

"Do you think Francis had the concept of being a new creation?"

"In so many ways."

Just then walking next us, we heard the joyful sound of Giovanni's voice, "Are you coming tonight?"

"How do you do that?" asked my husband.

"Do what?"

"Sneak up on us like that?"

Giovanni shrugged his shoulders and grinned from ear to ear, "I'm stealthy!"

"We wouldn't miss going this evening for the world," I exclaimed, "but will you explain what it is that we are going to?"

"No!" He beamed at having yet another secret. "But when you get there, there will be a woman who will meet you at the basilica door to explain."

"Giovanni! Always so mysterious. Give us a clue!" demanded my husband.

"Patience grasshopper. Just wait a few more hours."

My husband threw his hands in the air mocking defeat. "Ok."

"Patience *grasshopper*?" I gave Giovanni an amused look. "Are you sure you're a Franciscan? Cause I'm pretty sure the *Kung Fu* monk was a Shaolin."[5]

"Yes, but he had a Franciscan's heart," quipped Giovanni as he showed us his punch-block-punch aimed at an invisible opponent. "Don't worry, I don't fight. It's just good exercise."

---

5. *Kung Fu* was an American TV series (1972–1975). The Shaolin monk on the series affectionately called his student "grasshopper."

"Well okay then." I smiled.

Giovanni stopped. We stopped with him. He ushered us to a bench. "I have another story for you. About Francis's understanding of the new creation that you were just talking about. Wouldn't you agree it isn't just humans that God makes new?"

I raised my hand in a vote of agreement, "Paul says so in Romans."

> For the creation waits with eager longing for the revealing of the children of God; for the creation was subjected to futility, not of its own will but by the will of the one who subjected it, in hope that the creation itself will be set free from its bondage to decay and will obtain the freedom of the glory of the children of God. We know that the whole creation has been groaning in labor pains until now; and not only the creation, but we ourselves, who have the first fruits of the Spirit, groan inwardly while we wait for adoption, the redemption of our bodies. (Rom 8:19-23)

After reciting the verses in unison with Giovanni, I continued, "My theology professor put it this way. Even his old mangy dog Snoopy was waiting for redemption."

"Tell us the story Giovanni!" encouraged my husband.

It turns out that for a time, Francis lived in the village of Gubbio where a large, vicious wolf had started coming to the city. This wolf represented the brokenness of creation—as Paul said, creation is "in bondage to decay." The wolf, like us, was a part of God's beautiful creation that had gone bad. The wolf was so terrible and fierce that he not only devoured the pets and livestock of the city, but people too. Obviously, the villagers were terrified. They actually wore armor anytime they left their homes and even then dared not go outside the city walls. For even the armor did not protect them against this monstrous wolf.

Francis felt compassion for the people of Gubbio, but also for the wolf. So one day, after making the sign of the cross and announcing his confidence in God to protect him, he ventured outside the city walls to meet the wolf. The villagers followed from a safe distance, watching what would happen.

Upon seeing Francis, the wolf ran at him with his jaws open, ready to devour him. But as the wolf approached, Francis said, "I command you, in the name of Christ, to harm neither me nor anyone else."[6] The wolf,

---

6. Brother Ugolino, *The Complete St. Francis*, 310-312.

immediately at hearing the name of Christ, stopped running, closed his jaws, and approached Francis meekly, lying down at his feet.

Turning to my husband I exclaimed, "Using Paul's vocabulary, the wolf 'heard faith' when he heard the name of Christ!"[7]

Giovanni clapped at the connection with Paul. "Francis would agree!"

Then Francis went on to name the egregious sins of the wolf and offered him forgiveness. Having heard Francis's words, the wolf bowed his head. Francis took this as a sign of repentance and invited the wolf into the village.

"Brother Wolf, I command thee, in the name of Christ, to follow me immediately, without hesitation or doubting, that we may go together to ratify this peace which we have concluded in the name of God."[8]

That day, the village and the wolf entered into an agreement to live together in peace. Afterwards, the wolf lived with the people of Gubbio and they fed him from their tables until the day the wolf died peacefully.

"Is that true?" asked my husband skeptically.

I laughed while Giovanni went on, "Well, in the 1800s, during renovations of Chiesa di San Francesco della Pace in Gubbio, the skeleton of a large she-wolf was found under a slab near the church wall and was re-buried inside the church.[9] However, my point, dear friends, is that the redemption of the wolf—her transformation from evil to good—represents Francis's understanding of a new creation. It isn't different from Paul's understanding.

"The new creation was (and is) an act of the Holy Spirit working in all creation, including the life of the wolf, in order to fill the world with peace," I summarized.

With the end of the story and our promise we would see him that evening, Giovanni left. We meandered here and there soaking up everything. As the sun began to set and colors of pink and gold filled the sky, we changed into the one smart set of clothing we had packed. Then we caught our taxi into the valley. Upon arrival, the Basilica di Santa Maria degli Angeli did not seem to be open.[10] It appeared to be quite dark inside.

---

7. See the discussion about "hearing faith" in chapter 9, proof 1.

8. Brother Ugolino, *The Little Flowers of St. Francis*, 88–90.

9. This story is told on the website of the Church of St. Francis of Peace. See http://www.sanfrancescodellapace.it/storia/. "Storia." Chiesa di San Francesco della Pace di Gubbio (blog). Accessed May 24, 2018.

10. See picture 40 in the appendix.

We wrapped our way around into the courtyard where a very attractive, petite woman likely in her mid-thirties awaited us.

She approached us, "You are friends of Giovanni? Here for the *ricordiamo* Mass?"

She kissed us both and motioned toward the entry. But before she could usher us inside, we peppered her with questions.

"Giovanni said you would have questions. We have a few minutes, why don't we stand out here and talk for a moment. The short Mass itself will take place in the Porziuncola. It will be in Italian. The friars will stand or kneel on the floor, but we will sit in the single-person pew kneelers in the back of the chapel."

We learned that unlike in Francis's day, there are now various sects of Franciscan orders. Over the years, some broke away from the main line of Franciscans for a variety of reasons. Sometimes reform movements would return to following Francis's original rule—or to take on special missions. Other sects even formed independently from the original Franciscans. The different sects wear different styles or different colors other than the commonly known brown habit—some wear grey and even blue. Some tie their cord belts with knots indicating their particular observances. All honor Francis as their patron father.

"Giovanni, or as you will come to know him tonight, Brother Matthew, is a friar in one of those annexes," explained the woman with her long black hair fluttering in the wind and an expensive wine-colored pashmina wrapped around her shoulders.

"So, Brother Matthew." It was hard to call Giovanni by any other name, but I gave it a go, "is part of one of the groups that has returned to a strict adherence to Francis's rule?" I asked.

"No. Just the opposite. They are a sect that embraces the freedom you and Brother Matthew have been discussing. But at the same time, they hold the blessed Francis's desire to serve God in highest honor."

It turned out Brother Matthew's sect lives in simplicity, but not poverty. Similar to other Franciscans, their order revolves around serving anyone in physical or spiritual need. Imitating Francis's desire to serve God was their priority, not following his strict rule of life.

"Every year Brother Matthew's order picks a friar to live for one year as Francis lived. This is for *ricordiamo*—or remembrance. The one chosen is tasked with remembering the hardships Francis was willing to endure because of his abundant desire to please God. Tonight Brother Matthew will be decommissioned and a new Giovanni will be commissioned. Then Brother Matthew will travel to hermitages and monasteries and any churches that will have him to tell about his year in and around Assisi."

"And we have been invited to witness this changing of the guard?"

"Yes you have! As have I. By the way, I am Angela, Matthew's sister."

"You are a nun?" I asked confused. Her expensive black sheath dress, silver jewelry, and high-heeled leather pumps certainly didn't lean that way.

"No, I'm his real flesh and blood sister. I'm a lawyer and I live New York City. We come from a big Italian family whom I'm representing here tonight. I think we should go inside now."

My husband held open the heavy doors to the basilica. The Porziuncola stood under the dome of the basilica at quite a distance in front of us. It was lit with candles from within and glowing beautifully in the dark. We could hear movement echoing from inside.[11]

One could not enter this space without feeling overwhelmed with a deep reverence. We walked in silence to the arched door of the little church. Francis had called this place *la testa e la madre* or the head and mother of the Franciscan movement. Above the door of the Porziuncola was an insignia written in Latin: *haec est porta vitae eternae* or this is the gate of everlasting life.

We walked the long aisle and entered the humble little chapel covered with magnificent nineteenth century frescos. No sooner had we sat down when a procession of five Franciscan monks, dressed in dark brown robes with long front bibs and pointy hoods, passed us on their way toward the altar. They kneeled, not at the altar, but on the floor in front of it making way for Giovanni, who was smiling ear to ear as usual. He was still in bare feet and dressed in his potato sack cassock covered with patches. He kneeled at the altar. After a long time of silent prayer, a priest entered from the door on the right side and celebrated the Eucharist with the men.

Afterwards, Giovanni stood and turned to the monks who stayed kneeling. Giovanni spoke to them in Italian. At the end of his oration, he looked at us. There we were in the back of the tiny chapel with eyes wide, determined not to miss a thing. Speaking in English to us, he said loudly and joyfully, "The Christian life is lived to the fullest by letting the wisdom of the Spirit lead us and the strength of the Spirit enable us. Francis, with his great desire to please God, got a lot of things right."

---

11. See picture 41 in the appendix.

The friar who would now take on the role of being Giovanni for the next year changed out of his crisp brown robe, donning a fresh unpatched sackcloth. He removed his shoes too. Everything was folded and placed into a linen bag and tied shut. Simultaneously, our Giovanni removed his tattered robe and a linen bag was untied. A rich brown robe like the one the other brothers wore was removed from it. Giovanni put it on, then knelt and washed the feet of the friar taking his place.

That was the last time we saw Giovanni.

The next morning we were on the train back to Rome. Our pilgrimage had not produced the specifics of how we would lead the Christian life. Several big decisions still lay ahead of us. We had no next steps and no road map. Yet, it had produced something better.

We now knew the source of the wisdom—the one who would inform our daily lives, as well as our big decisions—was the Holy Spirit. That same Spirit would empower us to do the work God would give us to do. This Spirit—its wisdom and power—was both a promise and a gift from God.[12]

We also knew we needed to sow to the Spirit. On the train ride, we brainstormed together about how to do that sowing after we got home and back to our busy lives. We would set aside an intentional time every day just to listen to the Spirit—not to talk, not to study, just to be still and let the Spirit speak into our thoughts. We had learned our own baggage—things we accepted as truth, but weren't, and desires we had that weren't appropriate for where the Spirit was calling us—could get in the way of hearing the Spirit. We needed to watch out for these things, confess them, let God move the baggage out of the way so we could hear clearly. We had also been made aware that patience was important. We needed to be willing to wait for the Spirit to speak and to provide power. That power would sometimes come in the form of time and resources. We needed to follow the Spirit and obey, not lead—not take matters into our own hands. And we would seek out and find others with a common desire for fellowship and encouragement.

We had both fallen in love with St. Francis—his joys, his sadness, his achievements, his disappointments, his deep peace, his restlessness, his merry-making, his dark depression, his confidence, and his doubts. He was so beautifully human. Yet he was filled with the desire to serve God and others. He got an awful lot of things right!

12. Jas 1:5, 3:13–18.

Spiritual Practice 4
New Creation

FRANCIS WROTE THIS SONG in stages, adding to it as he grew in faith. It demonstrates the new creation Paul spoke of in Gal 6:15, Rom 8:19–23, and 2 Cor 5:17.

THE CANTICLE OF THE CREATURES[1]

Most High, all-powerful, good Lord, Yours are the praises, the glory, and the honor, and all blessing. To You alone, Most High, do they belong, and no human is worthy to mention Your name.

Praised be You, my Lord, with all Your creatures, especially Sir Brother Son, who is the day and through whom You give us light. And he is beautiful and radiant with great splendor; and bears a likeness of You, Most High One.

Praised be You, my Lord, through Sister Moon and the stars, in heaven You formed them clear and precious and beautiful.

Praised be You, my Lord, through Brother Wind, and through the air, cloudy and serene, and every kind of weather, through whom You give sustenance to Your creatures.

Praised be You, my Lord, through Sister Water, who is very useful and humble and precious and chaste.

Praised be You, my Lord, through Brother Fire, through whom You light the night, and he is beautiful and playful and robust and strong.

---

1. This is just the earliest stages of the song. The complete song is available in the referenced text: St. Francis, *Francis of Assisi: Early Documents, Vol. 1, The Saint*, 113–114.

Praised be You, my Lord, through our Sister Mother Earth, who sustains and governs us, and who produces various fruit with colored flowers and herbs.

Step 1

Find a quiet place—a place where you will be surrounded with nature, if possible.

Step 2

Read the scripture verses in the introduction to this spiritual practice.

Step 3

Pray the canticle.

Step 4

Meditate—dream—on what the new creation looks like in your life and in the world. Journal your thoughts.

Appendixes

Appendix A
Pilgrimage in Photographs

Photo 1: Our *agriturismo* in the Italian wilderness.

Photo 2: Chiesa di Satriano marks where the Knights of Assisi
left Francis to go find food.

Photo 3: Sunset with Monte Subasio on the left, the larger Assisi castle, Rocca Maggiore, in the center, and hang gliders overhead.

Photo 4: Path to Eremo delle Carceri, the caves where Francis would go to pray.

Photo 5: Eremo delle Carceri.

Photo 6: Left: Francis's cave. Photo 7: Right: Buco del Diavolo, or Hole of the Devil, where Francis cast a demon.

Photo 8: Last footsteps into Assisi. The dome of the Cathedral of San Rufino and the Torre del Popolo bell tower located in the Piazza del Comune are visible.

Photo 9: Left: Porta Cappuccini, the back door to Assisi. Photo 10: Right: Elders of Assisi gathering after church for Sunday lunch.

Photo 11: An Assisi street decorated with red geraniums.

Photo 12: Piazza del Comune.

Photo 13: Piazza del Vescovado where Francis renounced materialism by stripping naked and returning all his material belongings to his father.

Photo 14: Chiesa Nuova, a church built over Francis's childhood home.

Photo 15: Left: The parents of Francis. Photo 16: Right: The cell where Francis's father locked him. The sign above says, "His Father was a Pig" in Latin.

Photo 17: Delegates from cities all over Italy line up to participate in St. Francis's Feast Day parade.

Photo 18: The Knights of Assisi.

Photo 19: Left: Parade leaders. Photo 20: Right: Torre del Popolo bell tower and the
Temple of Minerva located in the Piazza del Comune.

Photo 21: Left: Basilica of St. Francis. Photo 22: Right: A delightful Franciscan nun enjoying the celebration.

Photo 23: Basilica di Santa Maria degli Angeli in the valley below Assisi.

Photo 25: San Damiano.

Photo 26: Left: The San Damiano Chapel. Photo 27: Right: The Finestra dei Soldi, or the Window of the Money, where Francis threw his money when the priest would not take it.

Photo 28: Street art celebrating Francis.

Photo 29: Basilica of St. Francis.

Photo 30: Mosaic of St. Francis above the arch of the entrance to the lower basilica.

Photo 31: Rocca Maggiore, the larger of the two Assisi castles.

Photo 32: Left: Cathedral of San Rufino, the childhood church of Francis. Photo 33: Right: A lion eating a Christian at the door of San Rufino.

Photo 34: Above the entrance to San Rufino.
Notice Brother Sun and Sister Moon on either side of Jesus.

Photo 35: Interior of the Cathedral of San Rufino.

Photo 36: Basilica of St. Clare.

Photo 37: The San Damiano Cross, which spoke to Francis,
hanging in the Basilica of St. Clare.

Photos 38 and 39: People of Assisi.

Photo 40: Left: Basilica di Santa Maria degli Angeli.
Photo 41: Right: The Porziuncola housed inside the Basilica di Santa Maria degli Angeli.

Photo 42: Assisi. Taken from Monte Subasio.

Photo 43: The author and her husband at the start of their pilgrimage.

Appendix B
Lesson Plans for Study Groups

STUDY INTRODUCTION

THIS STUDY GUIDE HAS eleven lessons. For group study, everyone will need their own copy of St. Francis and the Christian Life and a journal to record reflections. Even though there are only eleven lessons, you may want to carve out twelve meeting sessions with the first meeting, labeled as Week 0, for a time to get to know each other and kick off the study.

Each lesson plan has two sections: Preparation and Group Discussion. The Preparation section should be done prior to coming to the meeting. It will tell you which chapters to read and which spiritual practice to try throughout the week prior to class. The Group Discussion section is done together during the group meeting. Please start each meeting by going around the group and "checking in"—just a few sentences to sum up how each person is doing with the spiritual practices and what is going on in their lives. Then begin the lesson with prayer, read the assigned section of Galatians, and pick out the discussion questions that strike the most interest among the group and start with them. If the group gets interested in a certain topic, do not feel compelled to answer all of the questions each week. Then end with prayer.

WEEK 0: GETTING TO KNOW YOU

Preparation:

The study leaders will want to make sure everyone has a book of their own and a journal before this meeting. The leaders should read the above Study Introduction and be prepared to share it with the group. Some groups like to rotate leadership. If this is the case, assign who will lead each lesson. Some groups like to read the book through in its entirety before starting the study and then reread the assigned chapter each week. Do whatever fits your group's personalities.

Group Discussion:

1. Introduce yourselves and share why you have joined this study.

2. Go over the Study Introduction above.

3. Ask everyone to commit to doing the Preparations and Spiritual Practices before each meeting.

4. Ask everyone to commit to keeping conversations that go on within the study confidential.

WEEK 1: PILGRIMAGE TO ASSISI

Preparation:

Read chapter 1 and try spiritual practice 1.

Group Discussion:

1. God sometimes speaks through unusual people and in unusual ways (Exod 4:10, Exod 3:1–6, Num 22:12–35, 1 Kgs 19:11–12, Dan 5:3–7, Exod 13:21–22, and Ezek 1:1–16). Have you ever had this experience? What was your response? What do you think of the narrator's response to Giovanni?

2. Was Francis right when he said that the servants of God are like jugglers intended to revive the hearts of humanity and lead them into spiritual joy?

3. If you were going to go on a pilgrimage, what might be the question you would ponder as you walked?

4. St. Ignatius of Loyola, who lived several centuries after St. Francis, spoke of what he called consolation, which is the perception that we are moving in the direction God has for us. St. Francis might have called this perception peace. Consolation (or peace) gives one a sense of balance, contentment, and satisfaction. Do you feel a sense of consolation in your life?

5. Are you living the Christian life? If so, how is your life different from someone who does not follow Jesus?

WEEK 2: CREATING A COMMUNITY—GALATIANS 1:1-2

Preparation:

Read chapter 2 and continue with spiritual practice 1.

Group Discussion:

1. God called both Paul and Francis to particular demographics where they were to form Christian communities. Describe the demographics of the Christian community to which you belong. How did God call you to participate in this community? What gifts do you bring to this community? What do you expect of this community?

2. Does the Spirit guide your community? What tangible things does your community do to allow the Holy Spirit to speak to it? How could you increase the "visibility" of the Holy Spirit in your community?

3. Does your community follow a list of rules or keep a set of customs (spoken or unspoken)? What are these rules and customs? Are they just or unjust? Do they help or hurt your community? How should we react to unjust or hurtful rules and customs?

WEEK 3: FINDING FREEDOM—GALATIANS 1:3–5

Preparation:

Read chapter 3 and continue with spiritual practice 1.

Group Discussion:

1. It will become clearer as we get further into the Epistle to the Galatians, but Paul described his Christian transformation as being set free from religious rules and set free to be guided by the Spirit in order to do the will of God. On the other hand, Francis described his Christian transformation as being set free from materialism and set free to do the will of God by following a list of rules given to him personally by Christ. Fill in the blanks: Christ has set me free from _____ and set me free to _____.

2. Our pasts influence us for good and for bad. Paul was influenced by a difficult life of following a long list of rules and customs that enslaved him. Francis was influenced by a life of philandering and materialism that enslaved him. How does your past influence you and the way you know God? In what way does your past influence you in how you live the Christian life?

WEEK 4: CRISIS IN THE COMMUNITY —GALATIANS 1:6–10

Preparation:

Read chapter 4 and try spiritual practice 2.

Group Discussion:

1. Both Paul and Francis were convinced that Jesus had directly revealed the truth to them. In both cases, the wider churches of their era disagreed. Moreover, Paul and Francis would have likely disagreed with each other. From what you know so far, when it comes to living the

Christian life, who do you side with: Paul, Francis, Dominic, the Jewish Christian leaders, the thirteenth century church, or maybe some version of the twenty-first century church?

2. Paul and Francis were so convinced that they possessed the truth that they were unwilling to compromise. Paul was impolite to those who disagreed with him. Francis did not show the cardinal the respect this leader deserved and dressed him down publically. How do you feel about this? When is compromise appropriate and when is it not? When can you agree to disagree and still worship God together?

3. Paul said that if he compromised in this situation, he would be trying to please people instead of God. Are you willing to choose God when people will be unhappy with you? Is the majority always right?

WEEK 5: REVELATION—GALATIANS 1:11-24

Preparation:

Read chapter 5 and continue with spiritual practice 2.

Group Discussion:

1. Have you had a transformative experience where you came face to face with the living Jesus? Describe it. Don't worry if it is not dramatic like Francis's or Paul's.

2. What was your life like before you had a relationship with Jesus? Francis lived for the desires of the flesh. Paul lived to follow the requirements of his religion (and make sure everyone else followed them too). Are you willing for your old life to be history and to follow Jesus into something completely different?

3. Has God given you a calling or ministry? What is it? Note: Calls and ministries often evolve over the span of a lifetime. It is okay to have several.

4. Paul and Francis both started the Christian life on their own without supportive relationships with other followers of Jesus. Their authority came from God, not the church. Where does your authority to fulfill

your calling come from? God, the church, both, or neither? What are the benefits and problems with coming to the church instead of being a product of the church? What is your relationship with the church?

WEEK 6: REJECTED GIFTS—GALATIANS 2:1-14

Preparation:

Read chapter 6 and try spiritual practice 3.

Group Discussion:

1. Many Jewish Christians of Paul's day believed gentiles must be circumcised in order to be accepted by God. In reality, gentiles needed to be circumcised to be accepted by these Jewish Christians, not by God, who was offering them unconditional grace. Being accepted by a community is often a carrot held out to motivate us to conform, not a gift to set us free. What have others told you that you must do to be accepted by God, when what they really want you to do is conform to their way of life? What do you believe you have to do to be accepted by God?

2. Both Paul and Francis brought gifts to the church that the church wasn't ready to accept. What gifts have you brought to the church? Has the church accepted them? How can we accept the gifts of newcomers?

3. In Galatians, Paul was not terribly loving to those he had a disagreement with, but in Corinthians, Paul said to handle theological disagreements by loving one another and putting the other person's concerns above your own. Have people had theological differences in your church? How did you handle them?

4. When we trust God is taking care of us, we are set free to take care of others. A freedom that doesn't include caring for those in need is a bogus freedom. Paul wrote that he was anxious to remember the poverty-stricken Christians in Jerusalem. We have evidence that he carried through with this in 1 Corinthians 15:1–4. Is your community of believers exercising this aspect of freedom?

WEEK 7: ACCEPTABLE TO GOD—GALATIANS 2:15-16

Preparation:

Read chapter 7 and continue with spiritual practice 3.

Group Discussion:

Reflect on the following beliefs concerning religious rules:

- The rule followers followed the Jewish religious rules.

- The Christian leaders in Jerusalem followed four essential rules: don't eat meat offered to idols, don't eat blood, don't eat strangled animals, and don't participate in immoral sex.

- Francis had some essential rules he felt that the Franciscans should follow which included: don't handle money, don't own anything but your clothes, don't have sex, serve others, and attend the Mass regularly.

- Francis had a set of essential rules he felt those not called to religious life should follow which included: own only necessities, serve others, and attend the Mass regularly.

- Paul believed following any set of religious rules was the opposite of following Jesus.

Consider these questions:

1. Do you have a set of religious rules that you believe you should follow in order to live the Christian life? What are they? Where did you get this list of rules—did they come from God? What is their purpose? Do you actually follow them? Do you insist that others follow them?

2. In Mark 3:1–6, Jesus broke the Jewish rule not to work on the Sabbath by healing a man. On other occasions, he broke the Jewish rule not to eat with gentiles (Mark 2:13–17). He not only broke the Jewish law by letting those who were unclean touch him, but he touched them too (Luke 5:12–16). Can any of the rules you follow be broken under certain circumstances? How do you know when it is okay to break them? How did Jesus know?

3. If Paul was right and if following any set of religious rules is wrong, then how do you live the Christian life?

WEEK 8: CRUCIFIED WITH CHRIST
—GALATIANS 2:17–21

Preparation:

Read chapter 8 and continue with spiritual practice 3.

Group Discussion:

1. Paul taught that Jesus loved us and gave himself for us. Over the next week, say the words of Paul aloud, "Jesus loves me and gave himself for me. It is no longer I who live, but Christ who lives in me." Say these words several times a day in different locations. What comes to mind as you hear those words? Do they take on different meanings as you travel through your day?

2. How are you both crucified with Christ and alive with Christ? Give an example.

3. Do you live by faith in Jesus? Give an example. Would outsiders look at your life and see Jesus in you? Why or why not?

4. Paul taught that if we are truly living the Christian life, then suffering for Christ is unavoidable.[1] What do you think Paul meant? Does Christ want us to look for ways to suffer for his sake?

WEEK 9: PAUL DEFENDS THE GOSPEL
—GALATIANS 3:1—4:31

Preparation:

Read chapter 9 and continue with spiritual practice 3.

Group Discussion:

1. Francis's vision of God and the Christian life may have been influenced by the art and history of his childhood church. What about

---

1. Romans 8:17, 36.

your church's art and history influences you? What about your church might influence children?

2. How does being aware that the Holy Spirit lives within the followers of Christ change how a Christian lives? Do you trust the Spirit to guide your life or are you more comfortable with a set of rules to follow?

3. What do you think about Paul's proofs? Are any of them more convincing than others? Did they convince you that you should be living by the Spirit rather than by a set of rules?

WEEK 10: HOW DO WE LIVE THE CHRISTIAN LIFE —GALATIANS 5:1—6:10

Preparation:

Read chapter 10 and try spiritual practice 4.

Group Discussion:

1. What specific answers are you looking for in your life right now? How are you going about seeking answers? What question do you walk with?

2. Is there any baggage or past experiences in your life that keep you from hearing the Holy Spirit speak to you?

3. Do you trust the Holy Spirit to work in others? In yourself? Why or why not?

4. What are ways you sow to the flesh? What are ways you sow to the Spirit? What are some new ways you might try that sow to the Spirit?

WEEK 11: WHAT REALLY MATTERS —GALATIANS 6:11-18

Preparation:

Read chapter 11 and continue with spiritual practice 4.

Group Discussion:

1. Do you have the desire to do the work of God? What kind of limits have you placed around your desire? What kind of baggage do you bring? How can that baggage hinder you? What can you do to overcome it?

2. Do you have the patience to wait for God to direct you? Are you tempted to take matters into your own hands?

3. Francis had a night where he deeply regretted the choices he had made to serve God. Have you ever regretted serving God?

4. What kind of commitment can you make to spending intentional listening time with God? Make specific plans for a time and place.

Bibliography

Aquinas, Thomas. *Commentary on the Letters of Saint Paul to the Galatians*. Translated by F. R. Larcher, O.P. Albany, NY: Magi, 1966. Accessed May 28, 2018. https://dhspriory. org/thomas/english/SSGalatians.htm. Dominican House of Studies.

Barclay, John M.G. *Obeying the Truth: Paul's Ethics in Galatians*. Vancouver: Regent College Publishing, 2005.

———. *Paul and the Gift*. Grand Rapids, Michigan: Eerdmans, 2017.

Barrett, C.K. *Freedom & Obligation: A Study of the Epistle to the Galatians*. Philadelphia: Westminster, 1985.

Bettenson, Henry Scowcroft. *The Early Christian Fathers: A Selection from the Writings of the Fathers from St. Clement of Rome to St. Athanasius*. Oxford: Oxford University, 1969.

Betz, Hans Dieter. *Galatians: A Commentary on Paul's Letter to the Churches in Galatia*. Philadelphia: Fortress, 1984.

Bird, Michael F., and Preston M. Sprinkle, eds. *The Faith of Jesus Christ: Exegetical, Biblical, and Theological Studies*. Peabody, MA: Hendrickson Publishers, 2009.

Brother Leo, Brother Angelo, and Brother Rufino. *Legend of the Three Companions: Life of St. Francis of Assisi*, 1246. Kindle E-Book, 2013.

Brother Sean. *History of the Tau Cross*, Unpublished and undated paper by the Tau Community of St Francis, Monastery of St. Francis, Chapel Gap, Storth, Milnthorpe, Cumbria.

Brother Ugolino. *The Little Flowers of St. Francis: An Entirely New Version with 20 Additional Chapters*. Edited and Translated by Raphael Brown, 1958. New York: Double Day/Image, 1958.

———. *The Little Flowers*. In *The Complete Francis of Assisi*. 1226–1370 edited by Jon M. Sweeney. Translated by Jon M. Sweeney. Brewster, MA: Paraclete, 2015.

Celano, Thomas of. *The Francis Trilogy of Thomas of Celano: The Life of Saint Francis, The Remembrance of the Desire of a Soul, and The Treatise on the Miracles of Saint Francis*, 1228–1252. Edited by Regis J. Armstrong, J.A. Wayne Hellmann, and William J. Short. Hyde Park, New York: New City, 2004.

Chalippe, Candide. *The Life and Legends of Saint Francis of Assisi*, 1727. Translated and Edited by Hilarion Duerk. New York: P.J. Kenedy & Sons, 1918.

Dean, Judith. *Every Pilgrim's Guide to Assisi and Other Franciscan Pilgrim Places*. Norwich, Norfolk: Canterbury, 2002.

Dunn, James D.G. *Jesus, Paul, and the Law: Studies in Mark and Galatians*. Louisville: Westminster/John Knox, 1990.

Franciscan Intellectual Tradition. 2017. Accessed June 2, 2018. www.franciscantradition. org.

Giandomenico, Brother Nicola. *Art and History of Assisi.* Translated by Erika Pauli. Florence, Italy: Centro Stampa Editoriale Bonechi, 1995.

Green, Julien. *God's Fool: The Life and Times of Francis of Assisi.* San Francisco: Harper Collins 1987.

Guthrie, Donald. *Galatians.* The Century Bible New Series. London: Thomas Nelson, 1969.

Hawthorne, Gerald F., Ralph P. Martin, and Daniel G. Reid, eds. *Dictionary of Paul and His Letters: A Compendium of Contemporary Biblical Scholarship.* Downers Grove, Illinois: InterVarsity, 1993.

House, Adrian, and Karen Armstrong. *Francis of Assisi: A Revolutionary Life.* Mahwah, NJ: Hidden Spring, 2001.

Irenaeus. See Bettenson, Henry.

Keller, Timothy. *Galatians for You.* Purcellville, VA: Good Book, 2017.

Luther, Martin. *Commentary on the Epistle to the Galatians,* 1535. Translated by Theodore Graebner, 1935. Kindle E-Book, 2011.

McGee, J. Vernon. *The Epistle to the Galatians.* Vol 5 of *Thru the Bible Commentary.* Nashville: Thomas Nelson, 1984.

Merrill, John N. *Walking the Cammino di Assisi (St. Francis).* Hertfordshire, England: John Merrill Foundation, 2012.

Peterson, Eugene H. *Traveling Light: Modern Meditations on St. Paul's Letter of Freedom.* Colorado Springs: Helmers & Howard, 1988.

Sabatier, Paul. *His Life.* In *The Complete Francis of Assisi,* 1984. Edited by Jon M. Sweeney. Translated by Jon M. Sweeney. Brewster, MA: Paraclete, 2015.

———.*The Road to Assisi: The Essential Biography of St. Francis.* 1894. Edited by Jon M. Sweeney. Brewster, Mass: Paraclete, 2003.

Sanders, E.P. *Judaism: Practice and Belief 63BCE—66CE.* Minneapolis: Fortress, 2016.

———. *Paul: A Very Short Introduction.* Oxford: Oxford University Press, 1991.

———. *Paul: The Apostle's Life, Letters, and Thought.* Minneapolis: Fortress, 2015.

St. Bonaventure. *The Life of Saint Francis of Assisi,* 1250. Translated by E. Gurney Salter 1904, New York: Catholic Way, 2013. Kindle E-Book.

St. Francis. *Francis and Clare: The Complete Works.* Edited by Regis J. Armstrong and Ignatius Brady. New York: Paulist, 1982.

———.*Francis of Assisi: Early Documents, Vol.1, The Saint.* Edited by Regis J. Armstrong, J. Wayne. Hellmann, and William J. Short. New York: New City, 1999.

———. *Francis of Assisi in His Own Words: The Essential Writings,* edited by Jon M. Sweeney. Brewster, Massachusetts: Paraclete, 2013.

———. *The Complete Writings 1206–1226.* In *The Complete Francis of Assisi,* edited by Jon M. Sweeney. Translated by Jon M. Sweeney. Brewster, MA: Paraclete, 2015.

Sweeney, Jon M. *The St. Francis Holy Fool Prayer Book.* Brewster, Massachusetts: Paraclete, 2017.

———.*The St. Francis Prayer Book: A Guide to Deepen Your Spiritual Life.* Brewster, Massachusetts: Paraclete, 2004.

Vanchez, Andre. *Francis of Assisi: The Life and Afterlife of a Medieval Saint.* New Haven, Connecticut: Yale University, 2012.

Verdon, Timothy. *The Story of St. Francis of Assisi in Twenty-Eight Scenes.* Brewster, Mass: Paraclete, 2015.

Wiersbe, Warren W. *Be Free: Exchange Legalism for True Spirituality.* The BE Series Commentary. Colorado Springs: David Cook, 1975.

Wright, N.T. *Paul for Everyone: Galatians and Thessalonians.* Westminster: John Knox, 2004.

Wright, N.T, Mark W. Elliot, Scott J. Hafemann, and John Frederick, eds. *Galatians and Christian Theology: Justification, the Gospel, and Ethics in Paul's Letter.* Grand Rapids, Michigan: Baker Academic, 2014.

Made in the USA
Coppell, TX
21 October 2020